# Bulletproof Confidence: The Art of Not Caring What People Think and Living *Fearlessly*

**By Patrick King**
**Social Interaction Specialist and Conversation Coach at**
**www.PatrickKingConsulting.com**

# Table of Contents

## Introduction

Confidence hasn't always come easily for me. It's more than likely my lack of confidence started from my roots as the fat kid in class.

And when I say fat, I don't mean that I just had chubby cheeks. I mean that when I look back at elementary school class photos, I was literally twice as wide as the kids sitting on either side of me. At first I thought the image had been smeared and blurred, and that was why I appeared so wide. Sadly, my chins were there in sharp clarity, which meant it was a pretty accurate representation of my mass and volume.

I was large, rotund, and had rolls anywhere a little boy can have them — and some places they weren't supposed to. How do you expect that other children, insensitive and cruel as children tend to be, might have treated me? I was the butt of many a joke, and coming home holding back tears was a weekly occurrence.

Therefore, allow me to be a primary exhibit of how confidence isn't innate and can be picked up like any other skill, such as juggling or foosball. Confidence isn't a mythical trait that only some people are born with. If that was true, a fat kid from the suburbs certainly wouldn't be someone who was born with it.

On with the story.

At some point in high school, puberty helped me shed most of the excess weight I had carried throughout my life. My eating and physical habits hadn't changed, but suddenly weight was melting off my frame. With my jawline slowly emerging, people started treating me differently — both male and female. Anyone that's had a physical transformation can attest to the fact that treatment simply changes when you're in better shape.

And that's where an inkling of confidence can take root for many people. You walk outside and you receive positive feedback. Anything you attempt people are suddenly receptive to. This emboldens you to keep pushing your boundaries on the basis of these early, small victories, and suddenly you're feeling pretty good about your value as a person.

That was my first lesson in the realm of confidence — *the world we live in is shallow*. It just is, and as soon as you can wrap your head around that reality, you can start taking advantage of it in two distinct ways. But that's my story, and it only sheds light on a small part of confidence, because we all know confidence is not as easy as just losing weight and getting a haircut.

External changes can only take you so far and are just a piece of the confidence puzzle. But how do you gain confidence when you don't have anything to feel confident about? It's a serious chicken and egg problem with many people.

That's the problem I hope to be able to provide a solution to in *Bulletproof Confidence*. Confidence doesn't just appear out of thin air, and it can be fragile when it first shows its face. It must be rooted in reality, yet also recognize flaws and vulnerabilities. It's one of the most complex human states of mind, and people from all walks of life seek it for good reason.

As the saying goes, *all roads lead to Rome*, and it's the same with possessing a sense of confidence that is bulletproof, resilient, and makes you able to accomplish that which you previously thought impossible.

My hope is that after you read this book, you'll find your path toward real confidence, one that doesn't nosedive after a negative comment or after putting on a couple of pounds. It's a path that will scare you and may make you occasionally sweat from anxiety. You may need to examine some harsh truths about yourself and pull back the curtain on lies you've told yourself for years. But when you emerge on the other side, you'll still be living and thriving, and this is where real confidence is built.

When you are able to hold your head just a few degrees higher than you were before, you'll begin to recognize the importance and role of confidence in success. You'll be treated better and people will naturally assume positive things about you. You'll get further in life. It's not fair, but this time, you'll be primed to take advantage of it.

And hey, you may not even be starting from fat kid territory like me. Imagine how far you can get.

# Chapter 1. The Gatekeeper

It originally felt like a stretch to assert the following, but the more I think about it, the truer it becomes: *If you want to succeed in life, confidence is the gate you must walk through.* Period.

Whatever virtues you supposedly have, they don't matter if you don't have the confidence to make them visible. You can be as friendly as possible or the most interesting person in the world — but does a tree make a sound if it falls in the forest with no one around to hear it? Consider confidence the gatekeeper. Confidence allows everything that is good about you to shine through, and it also tends to obscure your flaws.

When I was a fat child, one of my hidden talents was that I was actually quite adept at comebacks to insults. I would mutter retorts under my breath that when they were heard, people would laugh their heads off. However, this talent of mine was never allowed to shine because I lacked the confidence to open my mouth and make myself heard. I felt so lacking in value that I wanted to hide from visibility and think about what could have been.

In the end, it doesn't matter what degree you have, how rich you are, or how great your hair is. Without confidence, they are nothing, because you will actively hide these traits from others. Things that should garner compliments and create a feeling of pride are things you'll want to hide because you don't want to draw any attention to them.

And ironically enough, *with* confidence, all of these factors are completely irrelevant. With confidence, you don't feel that you need any ornaments or ego boosts; you feel that you are enough as-is. For instance, we all have people in our lives who are impressive regardless of their lack of pedigree, and we all know people who have impressive pedigrees but underwhelm in real life. Interesting how that works.

The rate at which you get promoted, get dates, or succeed in life is influenced by your confidence quotient. Thankfully, confidence is the definition of learned behavior. At least, healthy confidence that isn't designed to compensate or hide something else is.

Confidence right out of the womb isn't real confidence. More accurate terms for that are arrogance, delusions of grandeur, hubris, and extreme narcissism. Sometimes the lines can be a little blurry, but there's an extremely easy way to tell which side of the spectrum someone is on. If their behavior appears fragile, defensive, and comes with a disproportionate reaction, it's arrogance, because the person feels that their house of cards is quick to crumble.

Positive encouragement is enough to make our day sometimes. It tells us we are doing a good job and headed in the right direction. However, a problem arises if you become dependent on such outside gratification to prop up your confidence. It's a dangerous position to be in when you are depending on sources other than yourself to feel valuable.

If suddenly that love and admiration from external sources were removed, imagine how lost you might feel. Confidence built by others is a losing proposition. You're building your house on a shaky foundation. You're constantly wishing and praying the twig that holds your confidence up doesn't snap in half.

For instance, if I insult Jon about his athletic abilities, he may laugh it off because he knows how much work he put into them. On the other hand, if I insult Robert about the same thing, he might lash out and immediately start defending himself. Which of the two do you suppose embodies truer confidence?

Jon embodies confidence as a process, which is a major theme of this book. Confidence as a process is incredibly strong because there is a body of work and evidence that supports it. This is the process of recognizing your strengths and flaws, and recognizing that neither of those — especially your flaws — define you as a person.

When you are fueled from external sources, you put yourself at their mercy and at their control. This is hardly a recipe for success. You will wither away without your source of strength, like Superman cut off from the sun. The only winning proposition is to build your confidence and self-esteem internally — this way, you are always in control.

Whether you like it or not, an invisible social hierarchy is formed every single time you meet new people. *Is this person going to be worth my time, are they valuable, and should I even care about them?* People examine a host of subconscious and barely-perceptible signals and make their decision in a split-second. You know this to be the feeling of "clicking with someone immediately" or "that person gave me a bad feeling."

When the signals you send out indicate a lack of confidence, that's a ticket straight to the bottom of the invisible social hierarchy. It's not that you should necessarily care what other people think about you — the lesson of this book is that you should care what *you* think about you. We don't live in a vacuum, though, so it's not about making the best impression on others, but about being able to create the world we want.

Simply put, how likely do you think you are to get what you want? How likely do you think you are to be taken advantage of or bullied? How likely is it that you will get ahead in life? If you're the bottom rung of the social hierarchy as a result of unconfident signals, your life is going to be more difficult.

If you project a high level of confidence, you will be perceived as being at the top of the social hierarchy, regardless of whether you actually are or not. People will treat you with more respect. People will give you the benefit of the doubt. People will treat you differently if you have a higher level of confidence. You don't have to be the most educated, wealthy, or smartest person in the room. You only need to send the right confidence signals and people will "read" into you all sorts of indicators of authority, credibility, power, and sexual attraction. This, of course, is the origin of the phrase "fake it 'til you make it."

We know confidence is beneficial for us to possess. But why do people respond so favorably to confidence?

When people see a confident person, it inspires them. Confidence is all about taking control over your reality. It's about you possessing the inner strength to impose your will to make "it *should*" or "it *might*" into "it *will*."

Most people are driven more by their fears than their dreams and aspirations. They're motivated more by pain avoidance than seeking pleasure. They don't want to fail, and they spend most of their time finding ways to avoid failing instead of thinking ahead and formulating how they can excel and soar. They react to situations to mitigate their losses and fears, instead of acting of their own free will.

Confident people remind themselves that they have the inner strength to make things happen. Confident people push the envelope. Confident people take risks. Confident people make that leap of faith. Confident people are naturally elected as leaders, regardless of titles and labels.

People's lives are a reflection of the choices they have made, and a confident presence reminds people of the *possibilities* in their own lives. It reminds them of what they can achieve if they make the right choices, and sometimes just the choice to be confident. It gives them hope. It gives them a role model to aspire to. At the very least, it's easy to be around someone who can take a joke, isn't defensive, and believes in themselves.

Imagine the opposite — how does an *unconfident* person make people feel? It makes them feel pity, negativity, or stuck in their own lives. Misery loves company, and so does a lack of confidence. We don't want to be surrounded by people that life seems impossible for — it depresses us, and at best, we grow tired of hearing people's excuses and justifications for not doing something about it. We want to spend time with those who point us to the freedom and strength we can choose ... not a proverbial Charlie Brown who constantly feels conquered by life.

If confidence can make people respect you and simultaneously make them feel good about themselves, it should be no surprise that confidence draws people like moths to a flame.

To move up in your career, you need confidence in what your abilities are. To upgrade your love life, you need confidence in the fact that you are attractive and that someone will want to be with you. If you are not confident, the world can be a hostile place. You might feel that life simply happens to you instead of you making things happen for yourself. It can be a downward spiral that can lead to discouragement, mediocre results, and ultimately, a wasted life.

Are you looking for a life full of victories and possibilities? Or are you looking for a life that is stagnant, mediocre, and essentially forgettable? You can either continue to make excuses or you can choose to start making progress by learning how to be confident. Begin by building a foundation for confidence.

## Chapter 2. Diagnose Triggers

I was recently watching a documentary on the mice that scientists use for experimental purposes. The mice were taught to run through mazes, swim, and push levers and buttons, all to examine psychological effects and what controls their actions.

It was particularly interesting because the mice, however sentient they were, were probably thinking that they were acting purely out of their own free will. They were making their own choices to push the lever, to run through the maze, and to perform whatever tricks they were forced to. It probably did not occur to the mice that they were being subconsciously manipulated into certain actions and behaviors, some of which were complex and required no small amount of effort.

For their actions, the mice were rewarded with cheese or other pieces of food, and then disposed of humanely in favor of new mice who thought they also controlled their destiny. Humans are just another type of mammal who think they control their own destiny.

This might be truer for some than others, but it's still a fairy tale that ignores the reality of past influences and external circumstances. We don't control who we are and how we act on a daily basis. Not consciously, at least.

We are but products of our circumstances and products of our times. We are born into the world as a blank slate, without a concept of what is good or bad. The events that happened to you when you were young impact your entire outlook on life as you grow older. This influence continues to rear its head throughout your life in positive and negative ways, especially in regards to confidence. You never know what small event caused a ripple effect that disturbs your confidence to this very day.

Where am I going with this?

Your confidence doesn't exist in a vacuum. You are going to feel small and vulnerable through ways you don't necessarily understand, and it's not because of who you are — it's because of what you've experienced in the past. At the very least, you need to investigate what might be triggering your unconfident beliefs so you can examine them.

If the mice were capable of logical thought, they may have realized that pushing a lever or button gave them food. Instead, they probably tried everything under the sun because they didn't see the connection. They acted with only a vague idea of what they were trying to accomplish, with no knowledge of how they were influenced. Again, that's how humans are with what makes us feel good or bad.

That's the first and foremost trigger to a lack of confidence. The past — circumstances outside of our control, how we grew up, and the role models we were exposed to during our formative years.

In fact, this can explain most triggers. It might not have been a traumatic event that caused you to forever view yourself as inadequate or lacking in a specific field, but there might be something you're unaware of that is causing you to feel a certain negative way or shy away from certain things.

A common example is when someone's parents criticize their weight from an early age, leading to lifelong body issues. Over time, this translates into a decidedly negative body image. Similarly, if someone's father continually drilled into their head that there is no second place, only the first loser, you can imagine how this person might approach competition and accomplishment. Anything you were repeatedly told as child is now an unmovable part of your worldview — for better or worse. It can be something as innocent as someone you know complimenting how attractive thin women are, creating an expectation that is either met or not. I'll leave it to you to think about what arbitrary truths you were told that you find difficult to live up to.

Overly critical parents can contribute to a lack of confidence because you may have been told you are inadequate, or held to impossible standards when you were younger. Children tend to adopt the beliefs of their parents and hold strong to them in the absence of a compelling reason to change. Thus, they go into the world with the belief that they are inadequate and perpetually lacking in one way or another.

Any relatively large failures from earlier in life can create such a negative association that you never want to attempt anything similar again. Past events serve to inform our worldview as to what is acceptable, possible, negative, and positive. There are so many moving parts it's almost a miracle if someone makes it out of childhood with healthy self-esteem.

Simple fear is another huge cause for a lack of confidence. In a nutshell, this means people want to feel good about themselves, but they are afraid of the consequences of doing so. It is typically characterized by a fear of rejection and failure. Rejection and failure by themselves aren't necessarily that bad.

Trying out for the basketball team and not making the cut isn't the worst thing in the world. However, it's the way your narrative must change to accommodate this rejection that makes us avoid it and act unconfidently. For instance, if you don't make the cut for the basketball team, what does that say about you? Likely that you are not that good, despite what you have always hoped or thought. There are very few ways to wiggle out of the conclusion that you are just not that good at basketball, aside from far-fetched ideas such as "the coach hates me" or "I was just having a bad week."

In essence, we fear that the rejection or failure will confirm our worst fears and insecurities, that they will confirm a negative narrative and let us know that we are indeed inadequate, whereas had you never attempted to try for the basketball team, you could still live in blissful ignorance as to your abilities.

Another illustration is something you will have heard on any night out. If you wanted to talk to someone attractive but lost your nerve, muttering to yourself, "They are too busy right now," "I'm tired," or even "They're not that cute, after all," these are all different shades of the same instinct to protect your self-image. Consequently, they make you lack the confidence to attempt anything that is even a little bit out of your comfort zone.

Even if you have the innate ability to do great things, if you're petrified of failure, you won't be able to take the necessary risks to get what you want. Often, this fear goes by a different name: the prerequisite. For instance, you could conquer the world, if only you could achieve X or Y first. This is a convenient defense mechanism that allows you to avoid taking action because you are perpetually waiting for something (usually impossible or unlikely) to occur first.

Ignorance is another powerful trigger for a lack of confidence. It's human nature to feel secure about what we understand and insecure about what we don't. It's much easier to swim in a pool that is only three feet deep versus a pool where you cannot see the bottom.

This fear instinct can often cause an emotional reaction where negative consequences are exaggerated, bypassing the accurate assessment of a rather benign consequence. Our imaginations tend to take fear and run with it, envisioning the worst-case scenario at the slightest hint of failure. This is characterized by exaggerated "what if" statements which detail only the worst possible outcome. When you know exactly what can and will happen, having confidence isn't so difficult, because you know there will be a minimal impact. If you're afraid of heights, no amount of logic can calm you down or stop your palms from sweating. Even standing at the top of stairs might set you off.

A final trigger for a lack of confidence is having your identity tied with something, then having that element suddenly removed or changed. For instance, the star athlete who becomes injured and can no longer perform at an elite level. Their self-worth may have been built solely upon athletic performance, and once that's gone, what is left? What can they hang their hat on?

If your identity is built upon being the best at something and you find yourself no better than average at anything, your confidence is going to take a serious tumble. You won't know who you are, and you won't feel that you have any value to people anymore.

A lack of confidence can take many forms.

At its best, insecurity protects our psyches and prevents harm. It lets you know what and who to avoid. It tells you to keep working harder and never rest on your laurels. It keeps you safe from physical harm. It causes you to double- and triple-check your work and demand high standards from yourself. It ensures you won't fall into the trap of overconfidence or entitlement. It will cause you to be humble to a fault and empathize with others who are also struggling.

And yet we would do anything it took to get rid of insecurity. We don't want to be subconsciously told how to act, we want to be able to choose whether we want protection or not. This is why it's so imperative to diagnose your triggers for lacking confidence. It lets you formulate a plan to deal with them so you can make choices using your own free will, as opposed to primarily avoiding the possibility of pain.

Ultimately, regardless of our triggers, it's important to realize how deep they can run and influence our thinking. The best way to understand the impact of low confidence is to contrast people with high self-esteem in social situations with people who have low self-esteem.

People who possess high self-esteem and confidence take almost all of the following for granted, and why wouldn't they? Shouldn't you?

*Socially confident people expect to be accepted.* When they meet strangers, they *expect* to make a good impression and don't get entangled in or stymied by fears that they will be negatively perceived by others. They take for granted that people will react positively to them. They never approach situations thinking, "What if they don't like me?" Instead they think, "I hope I like them."

They have the same adrenaline coursing through their veins when they meet strangers, but it manifests as excitement, whereas for others it will manifest as anxiety.

*Socially confident people evaluate themselves positively.* This is partially due to their healthy self-talk, and partially due to their positive self-perception. What does this mean?

They rate their social abilities according to a positive baseline. If they do well, that's par for the course. They expected that. If they do poorly, it's an occasional exception that they can learn from. They don't allow themselves to be affected by singular incidents that they know don't represent their abilities. They have a positive self-image.

*Socially confident people can deal with criticism.* Criticism doesn't crumble them. This is related to the previous point. Confident people learn to compartmentalize and separate criticism and recognize its actual purpose; they do not take it personally in an emotional way.

Their identity doesn't ebb and flow because of a single errant comment. It doesn't cause them to question their entire being or worth. They know they have worth even if they have faltered in a single area. In fact, they seek criticism because they know they need it to improve and they will be better off for it. They are not afraid that criticism will confirm a harsh truth about themselves that they've been trying to avoid.

*Socially confident people feel comfortable around superiors.* Define superior however you want — someone who is better-looking, more athletic, higher up in the office hierarchy, or more outgoing and charming. Socially confident people feel comfortable because they don't feel threatened, or that their flaws and vulnerabilities will be highlighted by the other person's outstanding qualities.

They can celebrate the talents and triumphs of others because they know that others' accomplishments do not diminish (and should not discourage) their own. They know the world doesn't run on an invisible currency that requires others to lose in order for them to win. In fact, they look forward to spending time with "superiors" because they know that's the key to learning and bettering themselves, as opposed to revealing flaws.

Are these simple aspects of interacting with others a given in your mind? In contrast, how do people who lack confidence approach social situations?

*People without confidence expect rejection.* Before they even step into a situation, in the back of their minds, they are already anticipating failure. They're looking for cues that people are disinterested or bored with them. They think twice before speaking and effectively censor themselves.

They are already thinking they will make fools of themselves, so they expect the worst-case scenario. This shows in their facial expressions and body language, and does indeed cause people to react poorly to them. They cause their worst-case scenario to come true because they never allow themselves to be vulnerable or open up to others.

When you expect rejection, you feel helpless, as if nothing you can possibly do will make a difference. Following that logic, why would you leave your home to try at all?

*People without confidence evaluate themselves negatively.* In stark contrast to those who are socially confident, unconfident people evaluate themselves from a baseline of negativity. If they perform well, they view it as an isolated anomaly. They shock themselves. They expect the worst from themselves and often get it because they have set themselves up to fail. Their preconceptions have, in their minds, made it okay for them to perform poorly.

When you set your expectations low, you skirt disappointment. That might provide a small level of comfort to you, but it means you will not strive to improve, and therefore never give yourself the chance to realize how much better life can be. In fact, higher standards scare low-confidence people. They're not sure if they will be able to cope.

*People without confidence despise criticism.* Criticism is a nightmare for the unconfident. On the surface they might want to put up a fight, but deep down, they feel the criticism is warranted and deserved. They can't defend themselves with conviction because they don't believe in themselves.

Their self-perception already hangs by a thread, so any small criticism can sever that thread and plunge them into an abyss of negativity. It's a crack in their armor that is representative of their entire value as a human being. Worse, they feel whatever shortcoming they've been attempting to conceal will be exposed by criticism. And then they will have to face the harsh reality of their failings.

Unconfident people will steer clear of the spotlight and taking action as a way of avoiding negative feedback, which might confirm their worst fears.

*People without confidence are highly uncomfortable around superiors.* Unconfident people are threatened by those they view as superiors. This is fueled in equal parts by jealousy, lack of confidence, and viewing social situations as zero sum games — there can only be one winner, so everyone else has to be a loser (including them).

Unconfident people feel they *have* to lose out in social situations. The worst part about this viewpoint is that they are more than happy to assume the role of loser. They feel swept up in a tornado when someone who is socially superior comes by. They feel discouraged and dejected because they see someone who represents something they can never be. Furthermore, they compare themselves to their superiors in a way that emphasizes all their own shortcomings.

The lack of confidence can run deep. What appears to be one relatively small shortcoming (lacking confidence) ultimately permeates how the unconfident person approaches their daily life.

A line is drawn in the sand as to where you can go, how far you can go, and what is worth your effort. As time goes on, this self-created circle of capability, competency, and confidence begins to collapse and shrink. Eventually, you'll feel trapped.

If you stay where you are, you're standing in a sealed room that is quickly filling to the top with water. You cannot stay there. You cannot keep running away from your social anxiety and fears. You need to act. If you don't change, nothing will.

You will have imprisoned yourself behind invisible bars. You can do whatever you want, but you choose not to because of those invisible walls — walls that were *not* created by people who have it out for you. There are no evil ogres keeping you down. Just you. Confidence can make you feel like the king of the world. But it's your choice.

# Chapter 3. Imposter Syndrome

I recall meeting someone who had four university degrees and was fabulously accomplished in life. I engaged them in deep conversation and walked away with the startling realization that that person didn't identify with their accomplishments, but rather lived under the constant belief that they didn't deserve their station in life.

Throughout the entire conversation, we talked about her coworkers and leaders in her field. Each time one of them came up, she started gushing about how intelligent and accomplished they were, seemingly oblivious to the fact that she was in the same sphere of status. It didn't seem like she was trying to appear modest or humble — it seemed that she truly believed she wasn't anywhere close to people she saw on a daily basis.

She just didn't feel like she belonged, felt that each day was another test she passed before people found out she was unqualified and kicked her out. She felt she had tricked everyone in her professional life to get where she was.

This is how widespread imposter syndrome can be. It can affect people who are the most accomplished, most pedigreed, and most prestigious because in the end, imposter syndrome isn't about actual value or worth; it's about self-perception and how you feel about yourself.

Imposter syndrome is a personality trait where a person feels like a fraud or imposter in the face of positivity or accomplishment — typically despite a wealth of information and facts to the contrary. In other words, they view themselves as incapable, untalented, and inadequate in most aspects. Therefore, if they find themselves in a position of power, their internal narrative becomes, "I can't believe people are listening to me. I barely know what I'm doing and I'm such a fraud."

Whatever is good about their life, they don't deserve it and have only gained their position through a combination of serendipity, luck, or some sort of mass delusion regarding their level of competence. Often, the more money, power, and respect this person gets, the smaller they feel. This is the paradox of imposter syndrome.

The conclusion is always the same: they don't deserve the success they have. In fact, they can't believe it, because it feels like they've just been making everything up along the way. Other people on their level, or even a level below them, appear to have it all figured out. But that's because they're making a faulty comparison — they are comparing others' best moments to their worst moments. It's like comparing a picture of yourself after eating at a buffet to a picture of someone else after they dieted and worked out for two months. Yet we can't shake the expectation that our worst self should compare to people's best selves. You're setting up a contest that you will never be able to win at.

Here's the secret to imposter syndrome: *everyone* is making things up constantly.

Not one of us really knows what we're doing in both the short term and long term. Imposter syndrome affects everyone to some degree for the same reason we often act against our own interests: logic doesn't compel us, emotion does. Logic would compel you to look at your external realities and recognize that luck doesn't continue to strike the same person so consistently for years.

By definition, that's not luck, that's being well-positioned to take advantage of opportunities. After all, the harder you work, the luckier you get — which brings us to the first point in battling imposter syndrome.

Remember your hard work.

Remember all the hours of sweat, blood, and tears you poured into something. For instance, take a professional soccer player. They are obviously talented, but so is everyone else on their level. To compete, the athlete must be in the gym twice a day, every day of the week. They've dedicated their waking hours to playing soccer since they were five years old.

Imposters don't do the hard work. They are just elevated suddenly, and they will usually fall just as quickly. You, on the other hand, have put in thousands of hours. You aren't suddenly being elevated — you are being recognized for your time and dedication. You've taken the time to reach a level of skill that can only be reached through time. Can others match the time you've put in?

We often turn to imposter syndrome because we rely only on isolated incidents of failure. These are outliers that ignore the hours of work that went into a task that goes well 99% of the time. If you studied for a test for weeks, you objectively have dozens of hours of studying under your belt. Dozens of hours of knowledge synthesis to draw upon that are thrown to the side on test day by imposter syndrome.

For instance, suppose there were eight years' worth of calendars where every day was marked with an X, and each X denoted that five hours were spent practicing soccer on that day. Would you be able to better identify all the work you'd put into cultivating your expertise then? All too often we discount our hard work and forget our role in our own accomplishment. Even if you're naturally talented, you've still had to work to harness that talent and say yes to the opportunities in front of you.

Similar to keeping track of your hard work, keep track of your victories, successes, and compliments. It's easy to feel that you don't belong if your memory is only filled with your latest failures, no matter how small. This can cause us to characterize a project, day, relationship, or skill as largely negative. Thus, remember your successes, victories, and compliments people have paid you. In fact, I suggest writing them down on an index card and either carrying it around with you, or putting it somewhere you will see it daily.

If you're an imposter, you're doing a great job if you're succeeding so much and getting so many compliments! If you are racking up victories and compliments, what is the practical difference between an imposter and someone who deserves to be there? Nothing besides self-perception.

Remembering your victories and compliments is important because the emotional power of a failure or criticism can stick with us for years. They can be all-consuming and disproportionately impactful, so you need something to balance things out and keep you on the right side of sanity.

One pitfall to avoid is allowing your perception to constitute victories solely as accomplishments of huge magnitude. I'm willing to bet if you hold this view, then you have a very low threshold for what constitutes a failure. In other words, it can be difficult to objectively evaluate yourself, so this exercise might be better done by enlisting the help of an objective third party.

This leads directly to the third point on beating imposter syndrome: Use objective measures instead of arbitrary measures where you will always come up short. Objective measures cannot lie to you, but you can lie to yourself every day.

Objective measures allow you to see your true progress and how you actually stack up to the other people. For instance, in basketball, hitting 90% of your shots is considered extremely good. One basketball player doesn't track anything and instead goes by how he *feels* his practice went. He has no clue how many shots he makes, and instead uses an arbitrary emotional measure. This player will have no idea of how he truly stacks up, and will be highly susceptible to imposter syndrome because he has no evidence of his skills.

Another basketball player tracks his shots meticulously. He hits over 90% of his shots the vast majority of practices. This player is not likely to suffer from imposter syndrome because, well, the statistics don't lie — only people do. Whatever objective measures of hard work and success you can find in your life, start using them and tracking them diligently. They are what you should compare yourself to, if anything, because they are the only thing that will illustrate your actual performance. No more hunches or gut feelings.

Next, even people who belong are wrong sometimes. Sometimes they are frequently wrong. Being incorrect from time to time doesn't make you an imposter; it makes you a normal human being.

Off the top of my head, I can think of one occupation that demands error-free work: a brain surgeon. For everything else, a margin of error is expected because everyone else has done the same. If Michael Jordan is incorrect about how a basketball play is run, does that make him an imposter of a basketball player?

No, it just means he had a momentary lapse of judgment, which everyone has from time to time.

Being incorrect and failing is just part of the game. It's natural, so don't make it represent something it doesn't.

Finally, try to see past titles, credentials, and degrees. The only thing those three words mean is that someone spent more time than in school. It doesn't mean anything about talent, knowledge, ability, or even intelligence. A PhD student is someone who spent at least five additional years in school, in which they typically study a very specific topic in their field of study. You are no less than them just because you don't have an acronym next to your name. In addition, it's not like you learned nothing in the five years someone else decided to pursue a PhD. You bring additional, different skills and knowledge to the table.

Imposter syndrome can rear its ugly head from time to time because humans aren't emotionless robots. However, feel free to pat yourself on the back and keep reminders of your success handy. Self-doubt can move quickly, so knowing exactly where you stand and remembering the work it took for you to get there can be powerful.

## Chapter 4. The Life-Changing Magic of *Doing*

One of the most paralyzing myths about building confidence and overcoming insecurities is the idea that you have to completely reinvent yourself — change in profound ways such that your newfound confidence may then be reflected.

Presumably, this cue is taken from romantic comedies where the main character must undergo a makeover to change his life, only to discover later that the change was inside his heart all along. There's nothing fundamentally wrong with this idea, because it has only the best intentions.

I've made the point multiple times that confidence must be rooted from within, it can't depend on anyone else, and it must be built through a process of small steps and victories. Enough with the platitudes and generalities — confidence doesn't require you to change your life, look, or repeat a set of daily affirmations each morning when you wake up.

Confidence is built through the life-changing magic of *doing*, taking action, making a leap of faith, closing your eyes and walking forward, and going for it. Stop thinking and planning and just reach for the unknown.

It turns out, contrary to what others would have you believe, we can't simply *logic* confidence into existence. Confidence is not a logical emotion, and you can't reason with it. It doesn't listen to your arguments and will steamroll you into fear unless you have a competing emotion to quell it. It's like the dog that just won't listen to your commands despite being trained for years. Therefore, *action and doing* and the subsequent small victories that ensue are necessary for building confidence.

Do what confident people do, and you will become confident. Some might recognize this strategy as being similar to *faking it 'til you make it*, but I shy away from using that phrase. In fact, I hate that advice.

First, it is reductive and unhelpful for most people. It's like telling someone to get better at surfing by *surfing better*, or a tall person telling a short person to simply *grow better*. It's meaningless advice at its core, especially if you aren't intentional about your actions.

Second, it ignores the root problem of why you feel a lack of confidence and only addresses the symptoms of a lack of confidence, which are general passivity and anxiety.

Finally, it's a solution that won't work for most people because they simply won't be able to do it. They either lack the mental fortitude and courage, they have mental blocks, or it's an impossible task. *Faking it 'til you make it* is helpful for no one, but taking action before analysis paralysis takes hold can change your life.

An important point of emphasis on applying the life-changing magic of doing is that you will feel uncomfortable and unready. At the beginning of this journey, you are never going to feel that you are fully ready to take the first foray out of your comfort zone, but that's just the thing. You can't wait until you feel like you have built up all of your confidence, because that moment will never come. You'll be stuck waiting forever.

For instance, if you want to attempt skydiving, then at some point, you just have to jump. There's no amount of rumination or preparation that will truly make you feel confident in jumping out of a flying piece of metal with only a parachute strapped to your back. The point is that you can't wait to feel confident before taking action. It's the successful completion of small, medium, and large actions that build your confidence.

Therefore, it works in an opposite way than what feels safe for us.

How many times have you withheld doing something you wanted because you wanted to wait until the day you felt fully confident to do it? The problem with this tendency toward feeling safe is your confidence will never increase unless you do the thing which you are avoiding. Ironically, that is exactly what will build it. And when you do it time after time, that's when your confidence really starts to grow. Make mistakes of action, not inaction, and force yourself to take action precisely when you feel scared and uncomfortable because that is the only approach that will truly work. There is no *perfect time* to do something, there is only ever *good enough*.

For instance, if you feel unconfident about your soccer skills (a common theme because it illustrates well), you can't just wait to feel good about your skills to practice new moves. There's nothing that would change your status quo, so you'll be waiting forever. Confidence doesn't quietly accumulate like your vacation days; something has to spur its growth. However, if you were to take the action-first approach, then you would practice new moves, feel embarrassed at first, and then slowly improve, creating confidence. Each time you successfully executed the new move and recorded a victory, your confidence would grow, and this would never happen if simple action wasn't taken.

A note — it's important to focus on the action itself, not whether there was a positive outcome. You can control taking a step out of your comfort zone, but you can't necessarily control what the outcome might be — at first. The soccer player shouldn't worry about how good the move is going to turn out, just that he does it.

Closely tied to the notion of prioritizing action over all else is author and researcher Stephen Guise's concept of *fearlessness*.

Fearlessness is the ability to do something despite the fact that you are terrified of it. Fearlessness ignores all negative consequences, while confidence is the understanding that negative consequences will be acceptable and unlikely. Guise posits that people would be more successful if they were to aim for fearlessness rather than outright confidence, because fearlessness gets more done.

Fearlessness allows you to jump off a building or approach someone attractive because you only need to suspend fear for ten seconds. Confidence doesn't necessarily allow you to do this. And most importantly, fearlessness allows you to take action sooner rather than later.

Confidence begins outside of your comfort zone. The reason you are reading this book is your comfort zone is too small, so you feel anxious more than you'd like. You have to continually take steps outside of your comfort zone to keep expanding it, or you'll be right where you started. As the saying goes, if you keep doing what you've been doing, you'll keep getting the results you've been getting. Nothing will change, and nothing will improve.

Taking deliberate action outside of your comfort zone and facing your fears little by little is what inspires confidence. It will give you the perspective to understand the possible consequences and bring them to mundane reality. It will also let you know that even if you make mistakes or fail, you'll still be fine.

Ah, failure. He who shall not be named, and he who shall be avoided at any cost possible.

What about the prospect of failure? This may sound counterintuitive, but failure is one of the best things that can happen to you. Failure is one of the best teachers you will ever have in your life, and its value will far exceed any successes you have. We successfully learn what not to do when we fail, and eventually, knowing what not to do becomes as valuable as knowing what *to* do.

Sadly, when we spend so much time and energy trying to evade and avoid failure, we end up learning those hard lessons later on. Instead of trying to avoid failure, look at it straight in the eye, learn what you need to learn, and move on. Don't spend your time trying to stay afloat just to avoid failure. That just leads to half-measures and won't teach you much about yourself.

For example, meticulously pick apart why you failed in a specific social situation, and exactly what caused your confidence to tank, or otherwise not rise. Attempt to understand what you did wrong, what you did right, and what was special regarding the situation. You can then use this information so you can avoid making that same mistake in the future.

Come up with a pattern or theory of why things fell apart and what the solution is. Test your solution by practicing again and again with other groups of people. By embracing failure and divorcing it from feelings of alienation, regret, shame, and embarrassment, we can make great progress.

We have been programmed since early on to read all sorts of mental and emotional judgments into failure. Just because you failed doesn't mean you are less of a person. Don't let failure lead to an emotional shutdown that gives you anxiety or frustrates you. It's just feedback that something was out of place, and a veritable blueprint on how to succeed next time.

The problem with success is that you don't know which part of the experience produced the positive result. With failure, it's easier to break apart your actions and understand the patterns that lead to disappointment, discouragement, and frustration. Failure can be a stepping stone to greater success, if you let it fulfill that role.

Your level of confidence is a reflection of your relationship with failure. Most people are so afraid of *doing and failing* that it erodes their level of confidence. Unfortunately, the true, straightforward, and direct path to building confidence begins with doing, which will occasionally end in failure. The key is to do more, reduce failure, then repeat the process again.

## Chapter 5. Take Inventory

Take inventory — what does that mean?

In a grocery store, taking inventory is when you look at what you have in the store and try to account for everything. The purpose is to know what is currently in stock, what is needed, and if there are any trends worth pursuing.

Take inventory of your strengths and weaknesses, and you can accomplish the same three goals. You will be able to understand yourself as you currently are, see what shortcomings you have — if any — and examine if your inventory has any hidden data or trends.

In a more concrete sense, go through the exercise of taking a piece of paper, folding it in half, and writing your strengths you have on one side, and weaknesses on the other side. Write anything that comes to mind and stop after just a couple of minutes. You probably won't need a long time to do this, as you probably have a few things in mind already.

How did the lists turn out? I'm betting the weakness side of the list was where you focused most of your attention, and the weakness side was at least 1.5x longer than the strength side.

Why could I predict this? Because when people seeking confidence try to come up with strengths or anything else positive about themselves, it's incredibly difficult for them. The list almost always turns out pitifully short to the point of inaccuracy and being misleading. If their best friend read only their lists of strengths and weaknesses, they might not even recognize that person from the description.

People lacking confidence are typically far too hard on themselves and have a skewed perception of their abilities. They have a near-impossible task in recognizing what they are actually good at and bad at because everything is fraught with negative emotion. If they excel at something, it feels like an anomaly or luck. If they fail at something, it lines up with their expectations. In many cases, these weaknesses are imagined, and the strengths marginalized or justified away.

This laundry list of weaknesses is more a reflection of fear and past bad experiences rather than of reality. It turns out that many of our perceived weaknesses aren't weaknesses at all, they're just something we may have failed in once or don't have good memories of. In any case, you've discovered how you perceive yourself — lacking in ability and talent, getting by on luck. This might be the first time you've put your feelings into words.

Now you are going to do this exercise again, but here's the catch: This time, you are going to focus on your *actual* strengths and weaknesses. A strength is defined as something you are better than many of your friends at, or something you are objectively above average at. A weakness is defined in a similar way: something you are worse than many of your friends at, or something you are objectively below average at.

The lists should be just about even in length — for every weakness, list a strength to make sure that you are accurately describing yourself. If you decide to get a head start by importing some strengths and weaknesses from the first list — what does and doesn't make the cut? In other words, what weaknesses are you omitting and why? For greater objectivity, have a friend help edit your lists. Often, people will refuse to fill the list out objectively despite being given the new definitions of strengths and weaknesses.

What is the purpose of taking inventory of your actual strengths and weaknesses?

To change the narrative you have told yourself for years. The voice in your head has been a negative one, telling you what you can't do and why you're not good enough. But it's wrong, and this simple list is evidence of that. Taking inventory allows you to gain an accurate look at yourself, which will help minimize your weaknesses and normalize your strengths. In short, you will feel permission to see yourself in a more positive light than before.

We all have an ability, trait, or habit we can be confident about, one that maybe we're the best in the world at, even. It can be as silly as twisting your tongue or finding parking spaces, but they are all valid talents that give you value and aren't insignificant. We all have something to take pride in and that we would feel comfortable doing in front of a crowd.

By gaining an objective and realistic view of what you are capable of, you can base your confidence level on what is real instead of what is imagined. Obviously, everyone in the world has weaknesses and things that they need improvement on, but confident people allow themselves to identify with their strengths and positive aspects.

If you are honest with yourself, you'll know exactly what yours are. You may also have to battle a compulsion to be modest when listing your strengths. This is a classic coping mechanism that acts to lower expectations for yourself so you never feel that you fall short. In other words, it's an excuse. It's not modesty, it's another place for insecurity to take hold.

No matter how you feel today, always remember your strengths, talents, and past achievements. Nothing has changed to separate you from the person you were that day to the current day where you feel low.

Take inventory to build your confidence, because just like your achievements, these things are evidence of how great you can be and have been in the past.

To that end, there's a concept I like to teach clients called the Confidence Resume.

The Confidence Resume isn't a checklist of things you should tell others, it's rather for yourself. And just like a job application resume, you should review and update it periodically. The purpose of the Confidence Resume is to again change the narrative you have of yourself.

When you have this resume created, you'll be able to glance at it and instantly know that you're not the type of person you feel you are at the moment. You're more than that. You're above it, and you have the evidence right in front of you. Every single item on the resume is a fact about yourself, but you've probably suppressed or ignored them while constructing your negative self-narrative.

This is the information that shows you just how great you are, what you've done, the type of person you are, and how impressive you can be. If brainstorming this information was difficult, it's a sign that you probably have an *extremely* negative view of yourself. It's the difference between telling yourself you're a good person and being able to list five things that make you a downright impressive person. By having your resume ready for action, you'll be able to battle your inner demons any time you feel low.

It won't be easy to come up with these on the fly, but that's precisely why it's so important to construct this resume beforehand. You won't be able to think of these immediately, and some of these are buried so deep in your brain they'll never come up organically. So what exactly goes into the Confidence Resume? This is just a guide; you can come up with your own list, but this works for me and is a great place to start.

- 10 most notable accomplishments
- 5 most unique experiences
- 5 most impressive moments
- 5 things you've done that no one else has
- 10 things you can do that no one else can

You get the idea. You can keep going, but what we're doing here is taking inventory of your best hits and making them easy to refer to.

Looking at the list, which will naturally become impressive and interesting, you can start to realize the type of person you actually are. You're the type of person who climbs huge mountains and was pulled onstage at a Bon Jovi concert! This is the conclusion the evidence leads to. Any other conclusion is in your head.

Take the time to write these out and go over them regularly. I even encourage people to write them on an index card and carry it around with them as a confidence boost whenever they are contemplating taking action. You've done it before, and you can do it again!

## Chapter 6. The Myth of Perfection

I want to say this immediately: this isn't a chapter about owning and loving your flaws.

Yes, everybody has flaws and weaknesses. Our flaws, warts, and blemishes are what make us human and real. Additionally, people who appear to be perfect are intimidating and make us supremely uncomfortable because they remind us how far short we fall of the mark.

But none of that will help you feel better about yourself or help you understand your perfectionist tendencies. Here's the truth: perfectionism is an unhealthy behavior that occurs precisely because of a lack of confidence.

You might call yourself a perfectionist, or someone with extremely high standards for quality. You might even deem yourself a purist and someone who accepts no compromises. But that's all a cover. You're not seeking perfection, you're seeking shelter from the judgment and rejection you think will occur if you aren't perfect. You aren't driven by quality and mastery, you are driven by fear of the consequences if you aren't perfect. Your standards aren't the problem, it's your fear of what might happen.

For instance, if you are a truly a perfectionist, then you don't care what other people think about your efforts; you are perfecting something because of your own standards. Yet when we think about it, we are almost always bound by other people's standards and worrying about how others will perceive our efforts. If you call yourself a perfectionist when it comes to cooking and you spend hours in the kitchen, are you more concerned with the food being the way you want it, or people raving about it?

They are two very different reactions, and the former is one that actually focuses on perfection. Now ask yourself, which would you be more concerned about? You can care about both, but if your overriding worry is about the reactions of the people you are cooking for, it's clear that calling yourself a perfectionist is really just a code for *someone who feels they can't be less than perfect, otherwise they will get rejected*.

Thus, perfection is a twofold myth. First, it's a myth because you are chasing a ghost. Perfection in any significant quantity doesn't exist. Second, it's a myth because it's something you've been telling yourself that has likely turned out to be untrue. What else do we know about perfection?

At its root, perfectionism stands for something positive. It stands for high standards and a pursuit of excellence. Taken to a healthy degree, it will help you achieve your goals and accomplish all that you want. But perfectionism taken to an unhealthy degree makes it so people feel defined by accomplishments and goals, and anything that falls short is a massive failure. Your standards become so high that they are impossible to meet.

You have created a game wherein you are destined to lose every time, and your confidence will tumble as a result. Suppose Robert wanted to improve in his soccer skills. Robert only felt good if he made a shot 100% of the time. This is impossible, even for the most legendary of soccer players. And yet this is the standard Robert holds himself to. He is destined to fail every single game because he has set his standards so high.

There are two options for when he fails: will he feel bad because of his own disappointment, or will he feel bad because he feels others will judge and reject him? With the former, you can see how perfectionism is a disease that unnecessarily creates unhappiness. With the latter, you can see how perfectionism is an attempt to substitute confidence.

Being dissatisfied with anything short of perfection means you view life on a black and white spectrum. It's an all-or-nothing approach where if you aren't perfect, you are an utter failure. Clearly this is not how the world works, but if that's how your mind works, you can see how you are setting yourself up for failure.

Perfectionism is also about wanting absolute control over the outcome of whatever action you are performing. If you feel that you are at a level of perfection, you know the exact positive feedback and outcome you will receive. A lack of perfection opens you up to the uncertainty of negative feedback and emotional turmoil — and if you think there is a possibility for those to occur, you will grow very uncomfortable.

Part of the problem is that perfectionism is a good concept, yet executed poorly most of the time. Perfectionism ideally means that you only accept the best from yourself and that you hold yourself to high standards and never settle. However, many of us can sink into unhealthy perfectionism, which can prevent you from ever feeling good enough at the pursuit of a goal that is literally impossible. This is the kind of thinking that destroys confidence because you are destined to fall short.

A better approach is to pursue excellence.

Excellence is what we are actually trying to achieve when we claim we are perfectionists. It means we are trying to perform at our highest levels and become our best selves, yet accept the outcome, whatever it may be. Excellence is perfectionism in the best of cases and pushes us to accomplish what we never thought possible.

The difference between excellence and perfectionism is visible when failure is experienced. Perfectionism crumbles in the face of failure, whereas excellence accepts it and moves onto the next step. Excellence doesn't live in vacuum, and it teaches you to persevere and build grit. Also recall that failure is one of life's greatest teachers, and a natural part of existence.

Finally, perfectionism is counterintuitive in what it will allow you to achieve.

It will actually only allow you to achieve part of your potential because you will be focusing on perfection versus actual production or accomplishment. For instance, if you want to produce a perfect painting, you might painstakingly focus on painting each blade of grass in a meadow scene. This could take you years, and if you make a mistake, you might throw the entire canvas out and start over. What if the goal was just to paint a meadow? You'll never achieve it.

Perfectionism will cause you to willfully ignore the following and hamstring your own abilities:

- What am I actually trying to do here?
- What should I ignore more of?
- What does not matter?
- Am I spending my time in the best way?
- And finally, am I doing this because I fear other people's reactions, or am I doing this out of my own free will and adherence to my own standards?

If perfectionism is on one side of the spectrum, then vulnerability is on the other side. Surprisingly, it's the side that builds and shows confidence. Vulnerability is a concept about embracing your flaws fully because denying them is useless and harmful.

How does acknowledging your vulnerabilities and sharing them with others build your confidence? It seems so counterintuitive. Wouldn't you come off as more confident if you hid your vulnerabilities and weaknesses from other people? In a word, no.

It's more likely you'll instead fall into the trap of overcompensating behavior. We all know people who fit this description, and they are usually insufferable know-it-alls. They become defensive at the first hint of vulnerability and protect their egos at all costs.

Interestingly, the more open you are about your weaknesses and limitations, the more positively people will view you and the better you will feel about yourself. Take me, for example. I'm not saying that you like me, but people tend to let their guards down around me after learning I was a fat child. It's something I am comfortable talking about, and I don't let it define me. There are two ways I could approach this fact about myself: I could laugh about it, or I could hide it and become awkward and angry anytime it was brought up.

Which do you think people enjoy more and perceive as more confident?

As much as we like the idea of perfection, it is our imperfections that draw us to each other. It makes us human and relatable. It wouldn't be a stretch to say that your vulnerability might be your greatest gift. And as it relates to confidence, showing your vulnerability and owning up to your flaws displays the most genuine version of it.

Let's look at our friend the peacock for a moment.

He is one of the most unique creatures in the world. As you probably know, the male peacock has a very long and elaborate tail that is the opposite of practical. It limits his ability to run fast and makes him practically a bulls-eye for predators. It would be an understatement to say that the male peacock's tail is a liability, a vulnerability.

But that flashy tail serves another important purpose in the male peacock's life — to confidently demonstrate his presence and virility to females. On one hand, the tail is a sign of vulnerability, and on the other hand, a display of supreme confidence. Something that would literally kill the male peacock actually increases the likelihood that he will pass his genes on to the next generation.

There are clear parallels to the relationship between confidence and vulnerability in humans. The more confident you are about your shortcomings, the more people are drawn to you. It shows to people that you have things well enough under control that you can be public about your weaknesses. In the same way the male peacock appears strong and confident to female peacocks, when you admit your shortcomings, people are more willing to respect and admire you.

On the other hand, when you are uncomfortable with your flaws and attempt to cover them up in various ways, you make other people uncomfortable enough to question your integrity. If you are willing to essentially be dishonest about your flaws, what else might you be dishonest about?

When you are comfortable with your weaknesses, it shows strength. The reason why this paradox exists is because it sets you apart from everybody else. Everybody else wants to put on a show that they don't have these weaknesses and limitations. People are more likely to respect and admire you because you say what others are afraid to admit.

By admitting your limitations, you also enable others to step up and admit their own limitations. They may not verbalize them to you, but they admit it by being open to you. I can't tell you how many people have opened up to me about their various insecurities and vulnerabilities after I told them I was a fat kid. I don't wield that fact for that purpose, but it's always a natural instinct after they learn about it.

Perfectionism is a disease that is best battled by pursuing excellence, vulnerability, and realizing that the label of perfectionist is used as a disguise.

## Chapter 7. Prepare to Perform

Imagine a situation where you might not feel comfortable.

A speech in front of a large crowd, perhaps. You innately know that to feel better and more confident for your speech, you would need to spend hours preparing and practicing in front of a mirror to make sure that you present exactly how you want. Right before you go on stage, you would probably also engage in some last-minute behaviors to pump your energy level up.

It's second nature to go through these types of preemptive measures and tactics when we are faced with a specific hurdle we want to overcome. After all, the athlete only goes through this type of preparation when she has a race coming up.

If you lack confidence, why not harness this feeling of preparation and readiness for your everyday life? You can begin the process of building confidence with just a bit of preparation and planning. You wouldn't expect to excel at public speaking without preparation, and likewise, why would you expect to feel good in your daily life if you don't prepare, create rituals, and rehearse like you are going to perform? Many people lack confidence and live with daily fear, but don't realize they can do something about it.

If you were to come up with a reason why you lack confidence about particular aspects of your life, you'd come to one answer: a lack of control. You don't necessarily fear being inadequate, you fear what the reaction will be to your inadequacy because you won't be able to control it.

You're uncertain about the outcome, the consequences, and how you'll deal with the prospect of failure. The power is completely out of your hands and you just might feel you are sitting under a dangling sword. The enemy that you know is less scary than the enemy you don't.

What if you could make things predictable? What if you could do things to get an expected outcome every time? This is precisely what happens when you prepare for the things that erode your confidence.

Focus on preparation through repetition. Repeating the same action and practicing it over and over will reduce your uncertainty about it and bring you closer to the outcome you desire. People may not be predictable, but everything else can be.

What are the specific steps you can engage in to prepare for a speech?

1. You write the speech
2. You record yourself
3. You edit and edit
4. You gain familiarity with the venue
5. You watch yourself in the mirror
6. You try to memorize the script

These steps come to us easily and logically. When you plan and rehearse, you hone your skills and reduce the likelihood of errors. You increase the likelihood that everything will go as planned. In other words, you reduce your uncertainty and can feel bolder and more confident in this predictability.

If you want to be confident in any kind of skill or any area of your life, just focus on one thing: *repetition*. The more you do something, and do it in different contexts, the better you get at it and more certain you feel in the outcome. Repetition exposes you to mistakes and shortcomings so you can fix them before the point where you would be judged for them. It also allows you to focus on smaller aspects of your performance that will make a difference, if you can remove yourself from worrying about not flopping. You won't need to focus on just getting by — you can focus on the small flourishes that will enable you to really knock something out of the park. This will have a tremendously positive impact on your confidence level.

If there are nine steps to something and you are an expert at one through eight, chances are you'll feel pretty good about yourself.

You may recall from an earlier chapter that I prioritize *action* and *doing* over just about everything else. Rehearsal and practice are simply other ways of doing. You don't have to gain confidence through trial by fire. You can, through planning, leisurely and systematically work on your confidence.

Sometimes the small things make a big difference in how prepared you are for performance.

Something you might not have considered is to engage in superstitions from time to time. Indeed, it can pay off to do what seems irrational. Research (Biswas-Diener) has shown that grabbing good luck charms and engaging in certain rituals does increase your confidence. It's like a part of preparation — it can make you feel like you have the keys to acing steps one through eight. Engaging in lucky thinking actually made people perform better on cognitive and physical tasks versus when they didn't have their charms or rituals present. This reinforces the notion you are neutral in the world; you are only defined by your own self-perception.

Similarly, engaging in pre-performance routines has been shown to increase confidence and improve performance (Norton and Gino). These are things we have all done, from eating only certain meals or listening to the same song, to wearing the same shirt or demanding silence. Coincidentally, these can all also qualify as superstitions.

Whatever the label, engaging in these routines has been proven to create feelings of consistency, which means you are getting physically ready for battle. Engaging in the routine makes you feel calmer because it's comforting, tunes out anxiety and errant thoughts, and keeps you focused.

Overall, routines make life more predictable because, as I've mentioned, they are now part of the performance process, and you have mastered the first couple of steps already (your routine). It's like learning the first few motions of how to throw a ball — once you master the beginning, the rest becomes natural and even instinctual.

Start small, almost imperceptibly.

First, assume you have what it takes, even if you feel deficient and incapable of crossing the chasm. You will surprise yourself on a daily basis. This establishes the base upon which your confidence will rest. Assume that things are doable, doable by *you*, and you will be that much more likely to accomplish them.

Second, start in your comfort zone. Start with small and easily obtainable goals. Do them once a week, then once a day. Build upon them. Gain the momentum to build up to once a day. The more you do something, the more comfortable you become and the better you get at it — and, of course, the more confident you become in yourself.

Third, scale up the challenge. Challenge yourself every day with greater goals. Explore new actions of greater difficulty and with greater frequency, and farther from your comfort zone. You may not succeed all the time, but accomplishment isn't the goal; the act of making yourself vulnerable and growing comfortable with it is.

First once a week, then once daily, try to do the impossible. You may fail nine times out of ten, but it doesn't matter. What's important is seeing a new realm of possibility. And on the rare occasions you do succeed, you'll wonder what all the fuss was about.

Finally, track your progress. Create visual evidence of the progress you've made and how far you've come. Give yourself the greatest gift of all — perspective on why you must be confident. Track the smallest, most incremental goals you can think of. Anything resembling even the smallest win must be accounted for.

Incremental victories may not fundamentally change your skill set, but they do impact your confidence.

## Chapter 8. Look in the Mirror

At this point, it's clear that confidence isn't something that just grows out of nowhere.

Confidence, or the lack thereof, is usually grounded in something real that results in an emotional reaction to what life throws us. If it's grounded in victories and pleasant memories, then we have a positive emotional reaction, and if it's grounded in trauma and failures, then we have a negative emotional reaction.

We are highly influenced by our circumstances, whether we like to admit it or not. The world gives us feedback and we react to it. Ideally, we want the feedback to be mostly positive. This is why perfectionism exists and why we hate feeling vulnerable, because we feel that we'll receive negative feedback. Conversely, when people treat us with respect and admiration, we feel good from the positive feedback and start to develop a confidence in at least one area of our lives.

One of the major areas we receive positive or negative feedback on every single day is our physical appearance.

We might want to deny it, but the feedback we get from others on our physical appearances contribute heavily to how confident we feel. Unfortunately, this means we as well are influenced by shallow things, both in ourselves and other people. If we're honest, we judge people on their appearance in a way that we hope they don't do to us — but they do.

This might sound shallow or depressing, but it's how reality works. It's part of human nature, just like cockroaches and centipedes are part of the circle of life. It's a necessary evil. This chapter at the outset might seem fake, disingenuous, or fraudulent to you. Unfortunately, there's a reason that people who look the part tend to get the part, and why we judge books by their covers. The world we live in is shallow. There's no sense in willfully denying what makes the world go 'round.

This is why people walk around with a happy strut after buying a new jacket they love, or a pair of jeans that hug their hips just right. They feel great about themselves and are confident of the way they are perceived by others. This stuff matters.

Why wouldn't you capture that feeling on a daily basis? This is just another case of making the unpredictable more predictable — how people will perceive you physically and the positive feedback you'll receive as a result. Therefore, if you want to be confident, you have to look confident.

My final disclaimer for this chapter is a personal story of mine. You know I used to be a fat child, but I didn't tell you I also reverted back to a round shape in my early 20s. When I made the decision to get a new haircut and shed 20 pounds, that was the first domino to fall in re-building my confidence because of all the positive feedback I ended up receiving from others.

If you look the part, people will usually take that and run with it. It's also the low-hanging fruit of changing your self-perception. It's one of the easiest things to improve immediately about yourself.

Thus, learn about fashion, improve your body, and consider that people make a snap judgment about you in half a second and treat you accordingly. Overhauling your physical image is an essential step to confidence.

This isn't necessarily a book about making physical changes, but if you want to embark on a confidence makeover, your first stop should be the gym. If not the gym, any means you can start to be active and improve your body. Start with baby steps. Learn to integrate consistent exercise into your lifestyle because the progress your body makes will literally and figuratively allow you to stand up straighter. If you conquer hundreds of pounds at the gym, it's something else for you to hang your hat on and take pride in.

Improve your wardrobe. This may not be something you've ever given much thought to, but there are reasons that businessmen and salespeople dress the way that they do. They are projecting an image and trying to take advantage of the first impression to elicit positive feedback from others. Are you really dressing the way you want, or are you settling for your clothes? You don't need to spend a lot of money to overhaul your wardrobe; you just need to pay attention to what fits you well.

We've all seen those makeover television shows where someone undergoes a complete physical transformation. However, the actual haircut and new clothes are secondary; it's the ability for people to see themselves as worthy, valuable, and attractive that really makes them feel new and improved. It can be so empowering that it's like wearing a mask at

Halloween, where you feel like you're playing a role and can do whatever you like.

And yet many of us still won't want to take the steps of improving our physical appearance because of a stubborn adherence to, "I shouldn't need to change myself for people to like me" or "I'm just going to be myself and things will turn out just fine."

*Just be yourself* is fundamentally bad advice because it will cause you to resist improving yourself or adapting to your surroundings. You don't have to compromise your values in order to dress better, look better, and have people react to you better.

The way you look is just one half of what people evaluate you on; the way you carry yourself is the other half. This mostly refers to body language and nonverbal communication. If you've ever walked away after meeting someone and felt that something was *off* about them, it's because their nonverbal communication was either not calibrated or sending mixed signals.

Remember, when you act confident, people will perceive you as confident.

First, speak slowly and deliberately.

For perspective, the most common instance where people speak quickly is when they are nervous. Therefore, when you speak slowly and deliberately, you send the message that you are calm, in control, and sure of what you are saying. Additionally, when you choose your words carefully and avoid weak, hedging, or noncommittal language, people will be more inclined to listen to you.

To get started, channel someone who you perceive to be a confident speaker. Start by copying and emulating, then find your own style. For instance, speak like a political leader who is decisive and firm, and ask yourself what they would say in a particular situation.

Second, watch your posture.

People look for signs of strength and confidence, and posture is one of the easiest to spot. Tilt your chin up, stick your chest out, pinch your shoulder blades together, and don't minimize the space you take up. Control your environment and mark it as yours. If this feels awkward and boastful to you, it's a sign that your posture wasn't necessarily strong or confident to begin with. Imagine how Superman proudly poses after he conquers a foe and you've got an idea of what to work toward.

Closely related to posture is the concept of *power posing*, which was pioneered by Amy Cuddy at Harvard University.

A *power pose* is any type of posture that increases the amount of space your body takes up. Again, reference Superman standing proudly in victory. Cuddy found that holding such a power pose for as short a time as two minutes can increase levels of testosterone by 20% and decrease levels of cortisol by 25%. This has the practical effect of feeling more confident and less anxious.

Cuddy also found that what she deemed low-power poses, a pose that decreases the amount of physical space you take, led to a 10% decrease in testosterone and a 15% increase in cortisol. This has the practical effect of decreasing confidence and increasing stress levels — think hunching over, covering your body with your arms, slouching, or hiding behind something.

Thus, the way you position your body can make a large difference in how you feel.

Finally, use powerful eye contact. Eye contact is the simple ability to look into someone's eyes and hold their gaze.

Recognize the power and importance of eye contact and pledge to use it more frequently and for no less than one second. Realize it's the nonverbal equivalent of saying, "Hi, how are you?" which we would never skip when meeting a stranger. Treat it as a nonverbal statement of, "I am trustworthy and will probably not slit your throat later," which means people ought to feel safe and secure around you.

It can be uncomfortable, and even stressful to emphasize, but if you meet the minimum requirements for eye contact, all of the aforementioned will be rectified. Pay attention that you are meeting people's gaze and not buckling under the tension.

Look in the mirror occasionally and realize that others are seeing what you are seeing in a vacuum. Is this positive or negative for you? Pick the low-hanging fruit of improving your appearance in basic ways and start to reap the rewards of constant positive feedback from others.

If you want to feel good about yourself, you must like what you see in the mirror. If you feel like a bum, stop looking like a bum.

## Chapter 9. Mindsets

Confidence is as easy you allow it to be. If you want to gain confidence, there are many easy ways to do so. You don't need to pay a steep price and you don't need to subject yourself to all sorts of trials by fire.

Start by embracing helpful mindsets and rejecting toxic ones.

### Always Be Thankful

The first step to gaining confidence is to be thankful for being yourself. This may seem ridiculous because people with low confidence aren't thankful for being who they are. They wish they were almost anyone else, and that is precisely the reason why you have low confidence. When you're not thankful for who you are and for the skills and talents you have, you are putting yourself in a position where you can only be unhappy. When you are unhappy, low confidence kicks in.

Low confidence, unhappiness, and lack of gratitude all go hand in hand. When you short circuit this emotional process by choosing to be thankful for everything you have and everything you are, you lay the foundation to gaining confidence. It's virtually impossible to be unhappy, angry, or sad and thankful at the same time.

**Take Inventory Daily**

Everybody has talents and strengths. There is no person who is completely worthless, and no one is inherently better or worse than anyone else.

You are probably the best in the world at something. Honestly assess your list of talents and strengths and review them every day. Review your Confidence Resume. Remind yourself what you have to offer the world and change your narrative. Write your talents on a card and put them into your wallet so you can be constantly reminded.

## Inoculate Yourself Against Consequences ...

... because the consequences aren't nearly as cataclysmic as you think.

Whatever you are struggling with confidence-wise, think honestly for a moment. What are the realistic, and most likely negative, consequences that will occur as a result of some sort of rejection or failure? Not the consequences that are five steps down, or that you conjure from a slippery slope — the *realistic* consequences.

Give yourself permission to realize that if worst comes to worst, things aren't that bad. You'll recover. Most people won't remember; in fact, it's more likely that only you will. Let this give you confidence that failure will only help you and won't tear you down. Fear is often grounded in lack of experience and exposure, so look at the worst-case scenario and free yourself from the fear.

## Weigh the Costs

What would you do in your life if you had the confidence to do it?

In other words, what are you missing out on in your life due to a lack of confidence? It's time to weigh the costs you are absorbing versus the benefits you are receiving right now. You will undoubtedly realize you have much more to gain.

Currently, you are kept from doing what you want and being who you are because of a series of moments of discomfort. That's it. For instance, talking to someone attractive only takes five seconds of walking up and saying hello. But that's just a massive hurdle many of us can't seem to overcome. Therefore, the cost is possibly having a new friend or significant other, and the benefit is to feel better and safer for those five seconds in order to avoid five seconds of vulnerability.

You'll find you are costing yourself everything you have ever dreamed of for a benefit of mere seconds, minutes, or hours of comfort. Is that worth it to you?

**Seek Positivity; Avoid Negativity**

Seeking positivity and avoiding negativity are not necessarily the same thing. Seeking positivity is to look on the bright side of things and always attempting to find a silver lining to your troubles. Positivity is believing in optimism and the best-case scenario, while simultaneously preparing for the worst.

Avoiding negativity, however, is far different. It's hard to soar like an eagle when you constantly surround yourself with turkeys. In other words, if you are surrounding yourself with people who are negative and who hate themselves, this will rub onto you and give you less reason to feel confident. They won't encourage your feelings of hope and positivity, and will rather drag you down to their depths of despair.

You are the sum of the five people you spend the most time with, so choose them carefully. Is this positive or negative for you right now? Leave your negative influences and let your positive influences lift you up with their own successes and ambitions. Spend time with those who inspire you to become a better person instead of enabling you to accept mediocrity, defeat, and frustration.

It doesn't have to be overt negativity. Whoever you feel worse after spending time with needs to go.

## Measure Effort

Measure effort as opposed to measuring successful outcomes.

You can control your effort. The act of doing, as we've discussed, is of utmost importance. You cannot control what happens after your actions, but that doesn't matter, because what's important is for you to do all that you can.

## Kill Comparisons

Without fail, one of the surest ways to become miserable and lose your confidence is to compare yourself to someone else. Why is this?

Because we don't compare ourselves to our contemporaries or people we feel we are better than. We always compare ourselves to people who have accomplished more, are more popular, and who we see as superior. It's a sickness.

Recall that comparisons occur typically out of jealousy, which is then compounded because we tend to compare other people's best moments to our lowest moments. It doesn't mean they are happier than you or better than you. All it does is serve to harm your self-perception.

Comparison to others can only lead to personal unhappiness. Instead, compare yourself to what you could be if you had a higher level of confidence.

## "Settle"

This is another way of encouraging you to avoid the trap and myth of perfectionism. When you first face this dilemma, it might feel like you are settling for something and not representing yourself in the best light.

But consider that you are not settling; you are just holding yourself to a different, more realistic standard that will satisfy your purpose in whatever you do. Perfection was also going to satisfy that purpose, if perfection were achievable. Since it isn't, seeking perfection would only have resulted in a huge waste of time and effort.

Perfectionism is the art of beating yourself up because you don't measure up to something that doesn't exist. Understand that there is a vast middle ground between settling and perfection that is perfectly acceptable for any of your purposes.

## Let Go

There are many aspects of your life that you simply cannot control. Are you going to worry about those *and* what you actually control?

It's often wise to worry about what you can control, and none of us are completely immune to stress. But to worry about things you cannot control is the very definition of useless. Focus instead on the things you can control, and don't let other things damage your confidence. How can it be a reflection of you and your confidence if you can't control it?

You can control how you act and you can control how you respond to things. You can't control what other people think about you and you can't control the past. Let go of those things and focus on what you can control to increase your confidence.

Separate your life and obligations into two buckets: things you can control, and things you cannot.

It boils down to one simple question: Will any amount of worrying change an outcome you cannot control, or will it merely serve to keep you up at night? It's almost certainly the latter. By worrying and spinning your wheels on something with an outcome you cannot change, you are suffering unnecessarily — twice, actually: once from the worrying, and again if something negative does occur.

Chances are you are creating your very own perpetual state of anxiety.

**Make Decisions**

What is a common characteristic of low confidence? The inability to make decisions because you want to optimize them, or make sure people won't be able to find anything to criticize about them.

In essence, we wait as long to make decisions as possible so we can check all of the factors and pick the most judgment-free decision possible. It is over-analysis at its finest, and it will cause you to lose confidence in your instincts. You're always going to be second-guessing yourself — that sounds like a lack of confidence at its core. Therefore, get into the habit of making decisions more quickly.

Choose what to eat off a menu more quickly and decisively. Pick your outfits in under 30 seconds. Choose what movie to watch without reading any reviews or information about it.

Unsurprisingly, there are also negative mindsets to avoid. These are specific thought patterns that lead to low confidence. It's tough to recognize how damaging our own thoughts might be to ourselves without some outside perspective. It just takes shining a light on your negative habits and inaccurate perceptions to completely change them and smash through your fears.

## Magnification and Minimization

Magnification is when you give proportionally greater weight to a failure or perceived failure. In essence, you create the story in your head that all of your experiences end with failure. This is obviously untrue, but serves to cloud your judgment and make it difficult to objectively view your strengths and accomplishments — which, as I've discussed, is important to establishing your baseline confidence.

On the flip side, minimization is when you give proportionally lesser weight to a success or strength of yours. It can be seen as an overabundance of modesty, but you might actually believe that you have accomplished nothing. You may even believe that any success was not due to you, but rather was only due to a stroke of luck or other people's help.

This has the same effect of magnification where you cannot truly see what strengths you actually possess, which makes you feel like you have nothing to tie your confidence to.

Notably, magnification and minimization can occur when we compare ourselves to other people. Other people's positive characteristics will be magnified and their accomplishments tied to their skill, while your own positive traits will be minimized and your accomplishments tied to dumb luck.

That is closely related to another mindset to avoid: mislabeling. It may sound innocent, but it can be just as pervasive and damaging as magnification and minimizing.

Mislabeling is when you ignore the reasons for your successes and accomplishments. People will low confidence will more often than not label their accomplishments in terms of luck and other extrinsic factors, rather than intrinsic skill and attributes that would cause one to build confidence in that arena.

The use of mislabeling, when not weaponized as false modesty, can indicate a deep commitment to low confidence. You simply can't see things in terms of your own abilities and need to justify positive acts as a result of other things and people.

## "Should"

This is when you feel that you *should* conform to a certain standard, you *should* do things a certain way, or you *should* meet an arbitrary goal. If you fail to do so, then you have fallen short and failed to perform a duty or obligation. Again, you are putting yourself in a position where you can't come out happy.

Thinking in terms of *should* places duties on yourself that may not necessarily exist. Most of the time, they don't. Expectations create room for failure.

For instance, if you believe that you *should* be able to solve a math problem in under 60 seconds and you fail to do so, you have just directly undermined your math abilities and lowered your confidence in that area. Are the requirements you are putting on yourself relevant standards, or are they arbitrary and perfectionist in nature?

## Chapter 10. Get Stoic

What is Stoicism? Stoicism is a way of viewing life and seeing your place in the world, and it was originally put into words by the Athenian philosopher Zeno around the 3$^{rd}$ century BCE.

How does it relate to confidence?

Stoic philosophy argues that unchecked emotions are some of the greatest enemies of your happiness and confidence. Rationality, perspective, and practicality are what drive Stoicism, where confidence is a solely emotional weight.

According to Stoicism, you have the utmost free will in any circumstance regardless of what your emotions might tell you. There is your *emotional* reality and the *objective* reality, and you can choose which you want to abide by. You have more control of what's going on in your life than you realize.

It might sound fairly fluffy and abstract, but this chapter will illuminate why Stoicism was so popular among the higher classes in Greek and Roman culture, including the famous Emperor-Philosopher Marcus Aurelius.

It is the ultimate version of viewing life through a combination of confident perspectives, such as:

- "The grass is greener on *my* side."
- "My glass is always half-full."
- "We'll make it work!"

Stoicism Lesson One — Want What You Have

The first lesson of Stoicism is that the solution to your unhappy life is right in front of you.

Everything you require for happiness and confidence you already possess; it's just a matter of wanting them, instead of having the expectation of more.

In short, focus on being content and confident with who you are. When you want to be who you already are, your appreciation increases and your expectations decrease. If you are always reaching for something you don't have, you'll create feelings of disconnection, smallness, powerlessness, and worthlessness over not having them.

Don't take anything for granted, and don't root your sense of self or happiness in the future. Wanting what you already have will give you a sense of appreciation that will make you more grateful on a daily basis instead of feeling jealous, discontent, and stressed about your deprivation — there is no actual deprivation.

Stoicism Lesson Two: Everything is Neutral

The second important lesson of Stoicism is that everything that happens in the world is neutral

— every event and consequence thereof. Every event has a different effect on everyone, but the events themselves are neutral, without intent, and play no favorites.

This means that it's your reaction and perception that are responsible for your lack of confidence. If you perceive events to be negative, they will be negative. If you perceive them to be positive, you will find the positive in them.

If you are sitting in a café and a driver slams into your parked car on the street outside, you have a choice about how you will respond. It's a neutral event, and you can attach any set of emotions to it you want. No matter how you react, the facts will remain the same: Your car is going to need repairs or will have to get replaced. Where you go from there is solely your choice.

Your level of confidence hinges upon your reaction and perception of neutral events. It's your response and opinion about the event that either causes you tremendous emotional distress or leads you to a quick resolution. Taking ownership of your role in your level of happiness is why the same event can affect people in drastically different ways.

We don't have control over most of the situations we are put into, despite our best efforts. But we do have control over 100% of our reactions and responses to those situations. The world hands us a blank slate every morning; you are the sole writer and editor of what is written on that slate.

Some people will inevitably see the silver lining of a storm cloud, while others are overwhelmed by the smallest hint of darkness. Which will you be?

Stoicism Lesson Three: Turn the Obstacle Upside-Down

Stoicism is a particularly helpful tool in battling the confidence-destroying obstacles we face in life. This lesson is about how to defeat negative judgments and, as the Stoics say, *turn the obstacle upside-down*.

No obstacles are inherently negative, and should actually be seen as an opportunity for something positive and growth-oriented.

The most practical effect is enabling the sufferer (so to speak) to become immune to negative emotions. Instead, they force themselves to engage in alternative thought patterns to gain perspective and move forward rationally.

For example, imagine you are a nurse and you have a patient who is very cranky. The reason you approached this person is because you wanted to help them. But this person is being surly, doesn't want to cooperate, or even tries to bully you. In short, this person is being mean and nasty.

According to Stoics, instead of feeling hassled, or feeling that this person is making your life difficult, try to think of this person as actually helping you out. How can that be? Well, this person's behavior is giving you a tremendous opportunity to exercise new virtues that you should have more of in your life, like being understanding, patient, and compassionate.

Our life is full of teachable moments, like the parables of old or Aesop's Fables. Regardless of how negative a particular event may seem, you can always try to reinterpret it as a positive opportunity or look at the other side of the situation.

The more you turn the obstacle upside-down, the more you'll realize that there really is no such thing as good and bad. It all depends on how you choose to perceive something.

Stoicism Lesson Four: Emotions are Created Internally

Emotions come solely from your reactions and choices. They don't come if you don't summon them, no matter how negative something might be.

Everything that happens in your world is neutral. Since bad or good does not exist in external sources, it logically flows that all emotions come from within. Each circumstance you face doesn't necessarily come bundled with a set of emotions. The narrative or story we tell ourselves is what creates our feelings.

According to Stoics, this is just a reflection of the fact that all these conflicts start internally. These are just outward manifestations of that internal conflict of judgment or discomfort with the self.

The best part of all of this is that we are always in control with respect to our ability to judge, because it is within our power. Nobody can force us to make moral judgments regarding specific things that are happening in our lives, or the stimuli that we come across. No one but you can put desires and attitudes into your life.

Just Care Less

Perhaps the underlying theme of Stoicism is the beauty of not caring. This is not to say you should ignore everything that's going on in your life, or people's opinions. You should care about the things you have control over. You should care about the choices you make that impact your mindset, and ultimately, your results. Your reality and confidence are what you create in your mind.

When it comes to everything else — things outside your control — feel free to not care. Free up your internal resources to focus your time and mental energy on things that truly matter. Control how you view the world and choose a more confident life now.

## Chapter 11. Supreme Self-Esteem

Some people see self-esteem as interchangeable with confidence, but that's not quite the case. They are related and can be said to achieve the same goals, but they are different at their cores.

Developing a healthy amount of self-esteem is one of the crucial components of living a confident life and achieving the success you desire. Without self-esteem, you will find your emotional state highly vulnerable to external circumstances, leaving you devoid of the competence required to cope and persevere through the inevitable challenges life presents you.

The notion of self-esteem as a distinct concept was pioneered by Nathaniel Branden in his seminal book *The Six Pillars of Self-Esteem*. These six pillars are the basis upon which healthy self-esteem is built.

## What Does Self-Esteem Consist Of?

Before we discuss the six pillars of self-esteem, it's important to first know what self-esteem is. Whereas confidence is broader, Branden breaks self-esteem down into two parts: *self-efficacy* and *self-respect*.

Self-efficacy can be described as a having the belief in our ability to manage the challenges of life. People who have high self-efficacy are prepared for events or circumstances to go against them because they trust in themselves to be strong and competent in the face of adversity. Whatever comes, they can handle it because of their skills, talents, or perseverance. The world won't collapse.

Self-respect, meanwhile, is the sureness we feel in our personal worth as human beings, regardless of any other circumstances. We have a right to live and experience happiness, and people with high self-respect know this fundamentally and cannot have it taken away by the judgments of others. If you have a sense of self-respect, it follows that you will be at ease expressing your thoughts, wants, and needs to others.

Having strong levels of the two components of self-esteem doesn't guarantee that we won't still experience many challenges and low points throughout our lives. Instead, it equips us with the tools we will need to achieve what we desire rather than letting challenges turn into failures and giving up.

Our self-esteem is also self-perpetuating; in other words, self-esteem widely determines the success or failure of our actions, and the success or failure of our actions then impacts our self-esteem. An otherwise capable person having low self-esteem may give up after failing to achieve their desired outcome in the first or second attempt, thus reinforcing the idea that they must somehow be unworthy of the achievement they desired, or that it is unattainable for them. Inject a capable person with high self-esteem into the same situation, and they may persevere despite failing on the first few tries, eventually leading to success and reinforcing the idea that they are competent and worthy of achievement.

While successful people may be more likely to have high self-esteem, it's not in any way an absolute. In some cases, low self-esteem is a driving factor in people's success, as they are constantly working to prove their worth to themselves and others through their accomplishments. In these types of scenarios, individuals build their self-worth on a foundation of achievement instead of inherent value as a human being, and such a foundation is more likely to crack under greater pressure.

The question is whether the people in the latter category are happier and feel better about themselves — probably not, because they would be acting on anger, fear, and latent feelings of rejection. Self-esteem marries high achievement with a foundation of fulfillment and *not caring about what people think*.

So how can you build high self-esteem on a sturdy foundation? Simply understanding self-esteem and its six pillars will not magically give you self-esteem. With consistent discipline in your thoughts and actions to adhere to the guide provided by Branden through the six pillars, over time, you can increase your self-esteem and the associated benefits.

## The 1st Pillar: Living Consciously

Living consciously is simply growing in awareness about the reasoning behind our actions and the consequences of the decisions we make.

We practice this by interrupting our typical thought patterns and responses to external influences, and then evaluating our thought and behavioral tendencies. By becoming aware of our reality and why we typically respond the way we do to various circumstances, we are able to align our actions with our beliefs and values. In the instances where we are inclined to act in a way which isn't beneficial, we can then consciously analyze the situation and determine a more appropriate solution based on our value system.

What might that look like?

Let's say you got into a minor argument with your long-term significant other. At the end of the argument, your partner left and said, "I just want to take a break and get some time to myself."

For somebody with low self-esteem, this can feel like personal rejection by their partner — hurtful and scary. They may be unable to cope with these feelings, so they'll send their partner 50 text messages asking to talk in the hope of immediately resolving their emotional pain — ignoring the wishes expressed by their partner just minutes beforehand.

Living consciously interrupts this thought process before it leads to the destructive action which harms the relationship in the long-term. It means understanding that fights are natural and that they don't change the love that you and your partner share. And rather than taking your partner's need for space as a personal rejection, you respect their wishes and allow them to have the time to themselves that they need. It's not about you, it's about them, and everyone simply reacts in their own way that is unrelated to your self-esteem.

After some time has passed, your partner gets back in contact and is feeling much better, and your small fight didn't snowball into a big deal or even a deal breaker like it may have if you had acted without thinking through the situation clearly. By increasing our awareness of our natural responses in various situations, we are often able to avoid the regrettable actions that lead to negative consequences and a subsequent loss in our self-esteem.

## The 2nd Pillar: Self-Acceptance

Practicing self-acceptance means accepting our body, thoughts, feelings, emotions, and past actions, as these are what constitute our present reality. This acceptance is paramount in the process of personal growth, because without recognizing that which we are, it is impossible to go about improving ourselves. A person who accepts themselves is honest with themselves about their perceived defects or imperfections.

Through this empowerment, they enable themselves to overcome the obstacles preventing them from changing what they can change while letting go of the suffering of wanting to change something that is outside of their control.

How could self-acceptance lead to personal improvement for you? There are likely more ways than you can think of at the moment, and new opportunities will inevitably present themselves throughout your life.

You've likely learned about the psychology theory that bullies are simply reflecting their insecurities onto their victims. The big, bad high school bully might be insecure about their weight, so they pick on the little skinny kid for being so small because it makes them feel better about their own size.

Both parties would benefit immensely from self-acceptance here. If the bully were to accept that they are overweight and that it doesn't make them any less of a human being, that allows them to then make changes to their diet and begin exercising more so that they can get to a place where they accept and like their physical condition.

The skinny kid may naturally feel insecure about their size as well, and any response to the bullying which comes from that place of insecurity — whether it's retaliating or running away from the bully's words — will likely lead to more bullying. If the skinny kid fully accepts that they are smaller in stature and that it doesn't make them any less of a human being, they can confidently and unemotionally respond to the bully, effectively ending the bullying by not giving the bully the reaction that they need to feel powerful. When you don't act out of self-acceptance, you act out of negative emotions such as fear or pain.

As we continue on through the rest of the pillars, try to notice how they are connecting with each other in the big picture. Our two high schoolers need to live consciously to be aware of the harm of acting out of insecurity, and they need to then accept the things about themselves that make them feel insecure before beginning to work on improving them.

## The 3rd Pillar: Self-Responsibility

Practicing self-responsibility means taking full control of our lives, no longer allowing our personal fulfillment to be dependent on other people and circumstances. A person who takes full responsibility for their life enables themselves to confront the challenges they face head-on and overcome them.

No matter how unfair your circumstances may seem, being the victim is, in essence, saying that you are not in control of the outcomes of your life — those outcomes are controlled by other people. As long as other people are in control of your life, it is impossible to have a healthy level of self-esteem.

Of course, all of our circumstances are not controllable. If they were, we would have a hard time finding ways to make excuses — though surely many of us would still try. Self-responsibility requires focusing on the aspects of our life that we can control — our responses to situations or the way we take care of ourselves mentally and physically.

Here's an example all of us can relate to from our childhood: having that one teacher that made you hate going to their class every day.

A person who has a high level of self-responsibility will understand that they've been presented with an unfavorable situation, but they can still succeed. Such a person may make an effort to communicate maturely with the teacher about expectations and what it will take to earn a high mark in their class. If the student finds that they really struggle to learn the material from that teacher, they may study with a tutor or look up supplementary materials online. And in the end, no matter what grade the student receives, they can feel good about their effort to learn and succeed in a difficult situation, rather than failing and blaming it all on the teacher. Someone with a low level of self-responsibility would ignore help and blame anyone but themselves for their low grades.

Life will constantly present you with challenges and undesirable circumstances. Being consistently happy and successful requires embracing those difficulties and taking full responsibility for how you respond to them.

**The 4th Pillar: Self-Assertiveness**

The practice of self-assertiveness is being open and genuine about who you are, and standing up for yourself to fulfill your needs and wants; it is what enables people with high self-esteem to be at ease in expressing their thoughts, feelings, and desires to others.

One of the great things about life is variety and diversity of people. No matter what you think or believe, somebody somewhere will disagree with you. The safest thing to do is to be passive and simply not express any thoughts or feelings that are potentially controversial, or to be disingenuous about who you really are in order to win over the approval of whoever you happen to be interacting with at the time. This doesn't lead to happiness, and can lead directly to misery.

At its core, this pillar simply means being authentic: expressing ourselves fully and openly and leaving it to other people to accept or reject what we are putting out. The underlying message is that you are okay with either acceptance or rejection.

Let's say you are talking to a friend, David, who begins gossiping about another friend of yours, Amy, in negative way. In this scenario, your friend is doing something that neither of you would like done to yourselves. If you are an individual who practices self-assertiveness, you'll say something to this effect and stand up for Amy rather than indulging in the gossip, even though that may make David think that you aren't fun or easygoing because you didn't tolerate a little gossip. Whatever David thinks of you is less important than being true to your values. Of course, this is easier said than done in real life.

Each time we have something to say in an open setting and choose not to out of fear of what people will think, we are showing ourselves through our inaction that our thoughts and ideas aren't valuable. Attaining healthy self-esteem requires reinforcing that our thoughts, ideas, and beliefs are important, and the best way to do that is to express them.

**The 5th Pillar: Living Purposefully**

To practice living purposefully means to have goals based on our values and desires, and to make decisions and act in a manner which is oriented with those goals.

People do not simply happen upon achievement and success. Instead, they are aware of what is important to them, what inspires them, and what ideas deeply resonate with their highest values and beliefs. They set goals based on these things and then ask themselves how they can achieve those goals. They formulate a plan of action and execute it.

It takes effort and self-discipline to consistently execute a plan and attain our goals. We must think about how our decisions will impact our ability to reach our goals and choose the option which most aligns with what we want in the long-term.

An obese person who wants to become healthy must practice living purposefully. They know that they want to be healthy and fit because it would have numerous benefits in their lives, but they are in the habit of eating unhealthy food and not exercising enough. So each time they have the choice between a sugary snack and a vegetable, they must project the consequences of each choice into the future and act according to their long-term goals. By doing this consistently over a long period of time, you will be successful in attaining your goals, which will then reinforce your self-esteem so that you can set new goals and continue living the rest of your life purposefully. You'll feel that you are living *your* life instead of impersonating someone else's.

## The 6th Pillar: Personal Integrity

The practice of personal integrity is the alignment of our actions with our professed value system. The word "integrity" is defined as being whole and undivided, which means that our ideals, convictions, and beliefs are fully integrated with our behavior.

Being a person of integrity may not always seem like the most beneficial choice in the short-term. It can be quite tempting, for example, to pocket the cash you find in a wallet that somebody lost on the street rather than trying to return the wallet and its contents to the original owner. Or perhaps more maliciously, to cheat on your significant other while on a business trip because they will never find out.

But doing these things is a direct betrayal of our values and diminishes our sense of self-respect. Whether anybody else knows of these actions or not, how you judge yourself is of the utmost importance if you are going to have high levels of self-esteem.

No matter how big or small a decision may seem at the moment, consistently giving yourself a pass on living up to your own professed value system will lead to compounding impacts on our sense of self.

Practice what you preach, be an individual of personal integrity, and you will be constantly building and supporting your self-esteem through your actions. It takes a more nuanced look at the components of confidence and again demonstrates how ignoring what other people think is a process.

## Chapter 12. Cognitive Confidence

Take two individuals with the exact same skill level and circumstances in a given activity and the more confident one will consistently achieve greater success than their less confident counterpart.

Having greater confidence and self-esteem is extremely beneficial for people to be more successful, happier, and healthier.

To that end, psychologists have developed a methodology for increasing confidence and self-esteem called cognitive behavioral therapy (CBT). Because of the plasticity of our brains, we develop strong patterns in our thoughts, behaviors, and emotions. For people who struggle with self-esteem and confidence, these patterns are often quite harmful and difficult to break out of, causing undesirable mental conditions such as depression and anxiety. This is what keeps us trapped in our heads within prisons of our own creation.

CBT tries to help patients to develop personal coping strategies and improved information processing skills in order to deal with their negative patterns. It does this based on the idea that your cognitions, feelings, physical sensations, and behaviors are all interconnected, meaning that negative thoughts and feelings can trap you in a brutal cycle that eats away at your psyche — sometimes even leading to psychological disorders.

The main strategy of CBT is to teach patients how to deal with seemingly overwhelming problems by tackling them head on, not avoiding them, and realizing the true source (or lack thereof) of fears or negative conditioning.

That's why you'll so often hear successful people talking about confidence and being willing to fail. It's this willingness to fail and essentially face fears and design ways through or around them that will lead to both success and confidence.

CBT aims to boost people's confidence by throwing them into the deep end and challenging the key components contributing to low confidence levels — self-deflating thoughts and ineffective behavior. This interrupts the cycle of poor confidence and teaches people to think and act like somebody who is confident until the feelings of confidence become natural.

## Cognitive Restructuring

There are two primary methods for intervention in the cycle of low confidence. The first is *cognitive restructuring* — a technique for identifying negative cognitive patterns and untrue assumptions we make about ourselves and altering them.

Common untrue assumptions have to do with our own lack of competence in a given scenario, or with other people's judgments of us.

Anxiety and a lack of confidence are not merely poor thought patterns; they are the reflection of thoughts, emotions, and behaviors which are all inextricably linked. Altering any one of these individual components will affect the others in the system. When one or more of those components are negative, the negativity is reinforced in the others and a negative feedback loop is created, maintaining the state of negativity.

Cognitive restructuring is a treatment intended to show people why they are getting stuck in these negative feedback loops and what they can do to significantly alter their thought and behaviors patterns in order to remove themselves from the vicious cycle. By recognizing a negative thought pattern and understanding why it persists, we can react differently to it and steer ourselves in a positive direction.

How does one build their awareness about their counterproductive thoughts, emotions, and behaviors?

Generally, the first step of those methods entails identifying subconscious thoughts — the ones providing us with a continuous commentary on our experiences as we are living them. These thoughts are constantly affecting our moods because we tend to simply accept them as accurate reflections of reality and ourselves. Therapists teach their patients to view these thoughts in a different way — as mere guesses about what is happening, rather than absolutes.

What makes this new approach on our thoughts so important?

When we stop accepting the narrative being written by our subconscious, we are able to begin considering alternative points of view. Suddenly the cycle is broken, or at least altered. This leads to a more sensible and stable way of thinking about whatever it is that is causing us distress at any given time, preventing us from falling into those vicious cycles mentioned earlier.

For example, let's examine the case of 16-year-old Nathan, who just got dumped for the first time in his life. His now ex-girlfriend, Macy, told him that they weren't compatible and she was no longer happy in their relationship. Despite Macy's maturity and candidness, Nathan feels terrible about getting dumped. His ongoing subconscious commentary may eventually lead him to feel that he is unworthy, inadequate, unattractive, boring, ugly, and fundamentally unlovable.

By the time the next school day comes around, a sense of dread and despair has set in and Nathan's self-esteem has never been lower. This is an example of how a negative feedback loop leads to a lack of confidence, which makes it all the more difficult for Nathan to reach out to a friend for help, be engaged at school or work, or participate in the activities that usually make us feel positive. His lack of support will reinforce his negative feelings that he is unworthy and inadequate, which may make him want to isolate himself more.

What could Nathan do differently to disrupt this cycle before it becomes destructive?

He could look at the dysfunctional thoughts that are making him feel terrible and begin treating them as guesses rather than accepting them. What are other possible explanations?

Maybe Macy never really did like him as much as she said, but it's even more likely that her feelings simply changed over time or that she got stuck in a negative feedback loop thinking about the relationship. Perhaps it was really about her and not about Nathan, and he is actually still quite attractive. Perhaps she has her own issues she must deal with and is heartbroken at having to break up with Nathan. Perhaps it was all a misunderstanding. Whatever the case, the fault doesn't lie with Nathan's inadequacy, and though he still probably isn't looking forward to school tomorrow, the prospect is not nearly as daunting as it was in his negative feedback loop.

By simply considering alternative possibilities, we can balance out or emotions and thoughts and reduce the sadness and hopelessness that occurs when we get trapped in a negative feedback loop. This, in turn, enables us to engage in the behaviors and activities which promote our well-being, pulling us out of our dark mindset and making us stronger and better for the experience of overcoming it.

## Systematic Exposure

A second method for building the confidence is based on the fact that confidence itself is activity dependent.

Somebody can be fully confident while engaging in an activity at which they excel, while utterly lacking confidence in their abilities to do the things that cause them fear and anxiety.

Systematic exposure is exactly what it sounds like — a methodology for gradually exposing ourselves to the situations we would typically avoid, thus learning that those activities are not as bad or scary as our minds had made them out to be.

You see, when we avoid situations that we fear, we are reinforcing that fear and anxiety, causing it to reach ever more irrational levels and spread across other areas of our lives. The best way to break down that fear is by realistically evaluating if the thing we fear is truly worthy of the fear in the first place. In the vast majority of cases, they are not. Except spiders.

Exposure therapy has been shown to be a highly effective treatment for anxiety, with as many as 80% of patients experiencing substantial reductions in their anxiety after only a few treatments. Those sessions work by bringing the patient into contact with whatever they fear and sustaining that contact just long enough for the patient to observe that the negative consequences they expected are not actually going to occur, thereby weakening their anxiety.

The "systematic" part of the therapy is in how fear and anxiety are broken down. Before beginning the exposure process, a *fear hierarchy* is established as the blueprint for the treatment, listing the feared situations and activities and then arranging them with the least anxiety-provoking at the bottom and the most anxiety-provoking at the top.

Patients are then free to work at their own pace, leaving their comfort zones but not exposing themselves to anything they feel is too overwhelming. They start at the bottom of their fear hierarchy and work their way up as they establish more and more confidence through exposure and mastery of the less anxiety-provoking situations and activities.

Let's take somebody who is uncomfortable with social attention as an example, and break down their anxieties into a manageable hierarchy.

At the top, we might have speaking in front of a large crowd. In the middle, there are activities like making a presentation to work colleagues or volunteering to go to the front of the class and share their solution to a homework problem. Then at the bottom, we have less intimidating tasks, including approaching a couple of strangers and starting a conversation with them, or even speaking for a prolonged period to a group of acquaintances.

Our socially anxious friend would start off by talking to strangers for a minute or two, and repetitively do so until the thought of approaching a group of strangers no longer fazes them. At this point, they might begin speaking up more often when they have something to say at school or work, until the thought of being the center of attention of a small group of people doesn't induce anxiety. Finally, they could sign up for a public speaking class and purposely expose themselves to the fear at the top of their hierarchy, with the confidence of having successfully overcome all of the fears below it.

One of the major benefits of this is that our anxiety and fear for one particular situation or activity can often be a microcosm of the anxiety and fear as a whole, and so overcoming just one instance of it can carry over beyond the rest of that particular fear hierarchy and into the other areas of our life.

These methodologies of CBT can be powerful tools for self-improvement when applied well. Confidence is not something which you can suddenly attain by reading about it and understanding how it works. Unfortunately, few things in life are that easy. Building confidence will require a concerted effort to become more aware of your negative feedback loops caused by interconnected thoughts, feelings, and behaviors. It will likely also require systematically stepping out of your comfort zone one anxiety-inducing activity at a time.

In the end, it may be difficult or impossible to always be confident. If you are constantly trying new things and attempting to attain new skills, it's inevitable that you'll question your abilities at one time or another. But it can be endlessly beneficial for your life if you make the effort to experience all those things that cause you fear and anxiety, and to learn that they weren't so bad, after all.

## Chapter 13. Banish Your Negative Self-Talk

When I was younger, I vividly recall making a presentation on owls. It went poorly, to say the least. I fumbled over my opening sentence, tripped on the easel that was holding up my poster, and for the grand finale, I committed a Freudian slip and said that owls hunted vermin and rodents such as my teacher.

I sat down in a puddle of sweat to sparse and confused applause. The first thing I did was start berating myself for every little thing that went wrong.

*How could I trip? I'm so clumsy!*

*How could I mess up the beginning! I'm so bad at speaking!*

*How could I call Mrs. Robinson a vermin? I'm so stupid!*

The speech itself probably wasn't as bad as I remember it; after all, I received an A-. It was one of my better grades in the class, actually.

But my negative self-talk, based on self-created assumptions, scarred me and scared me away from giving speeches for years. The experience made me frame myself as "terrible at public speaking."

In one fell swoop, I had handily minimized myself. Not only that, I had extended the impact of one isolated incident to a degradation of my character as a whole. Because I hadn't performed optimally on this one speech, I was now an objectively worse person than I was the day before I'd given the speech. I couldn't see the forest for the trees.

That's the power of negative self-talk. We use negative self-talk to explain situations that we can't assess objectively. When we react emotionally, we feel helpless to control our fates and practically refuse to see the bright side of any situation.

The first step to making progress in addressing a lack of confidence is to pay attention to how we talk to ourselves. Everybody has an internal monologue that plays on repeat. Everybody is always making quick mental judgments of the things playing out around them or the things they are observing.

We're not always aware of it and it runs subconsciously, and that's what makes it so potentially dangerous. You never know how you end up with these thoughts until it's too late. That's how I ended up with a fear of public speaking for years afterwards — I didn't realize it stemmed from this formative experience and the associated negative self-talk.

If you have low confidence, it's because you unknowingly use negative self-talk to make judgments and assumptions about yourself and others. You do this constantly and the judgments are flat-out inaccurate.

You end up creating a narrative that is both damaging and disempowering. You feel socially weaker the more you engage in this self-talk. The worst part is you feel you can't stop, even if you can logically realize it's not reality. All it takes is one little thing to push you over the edge.

You can't control your feelings, and you feel this is completely natural and there is no other alternative reading to the things you observe. What's more, you have the tendency to extend a judgment on a small aspect of your life to your entire being and existence. "I'm terrible at speaking" suddenly becomes "I can't deal with people at all."

**Negative Self-talk Patterns**

When you say to yourself that you aren't good enough or there's no reason why people should choose you, you are engaging in negative self-talk.

It's important that you pinpoint and clearly identify negative self-talk and know how to tell it apart from neutral, or even positive self-talk.

As the old saying goes, "If you repeat something long enough, eventually, you might believe that it's true." Of course, a lie even repeated a billion times is still a lie. But it doesn't really matter if you believe it. Your *perception* becomes reality when you keep repeating negative self-talk. The more you repeat it, the greater this downward spiral of negative mental states and negative external social responses will be.

Think of your stream of consciousness as a Facebook timeline.

There are all sorts of things that appear on your timeline. If you just let your negative mental habits filter everything, it's easy to think that all the items on your newsfeed or timeline are coming from a negative light. They just reinforce what you already concluded about who you are, what you're capable of, and what your limits are in social situations, no matter how inaccurate that perception is.

These are all judgments and assumptions you've chosen to create your reality. You are subscribing to them and cosigning them. If you understand this, then you can take the opposite action, which is to edit what you choose to conclude. You can look at what you have been saying all along and contradict it or redirect it.

To make progress on this part, you have to understand the narrative you tell yourself.

Ask yourself: do you believe there's something wrong with you? Or that you're not good enough because of X, Y, or Z? Do you think you're not good enough because you don't have A, B, or C? And what do these beliefs say about your overall character?

This is not real.

These thoughts are arbitrary because everyone is different. People who have the same things as you, who come from similar backgrounds, and who share similar experiences might actually have completely different self-talk. There are at least two primary ways to look at any situation, and there are limitless alternate explanations other than you being incredibly inadequate in something.

## Self-analysis

When you think you can't do something or you feel you're making an excuse for something, the most important step you need to take is to *ask yourself why*. The same applies to when you fail to attempt something out of fear of failure or rejection. Why did you feel the need to say that? Why is there a causal link between what transpired and how you feel?

Where does it come from? Who are you hoping to make feel better? What are the alternate explanations that don't involve you being inadequate, and what does this mean about your self-perception? And is there actual evidence, or is it just an assumption you've made based on emotion?

It's likely this isn't the first time you've resorted to negative self-talk to explain a situation.

Are there distinct facts or experiences from your personal history that created the assumptions you are now laboring under? What happened in the past for you to be conditioned to react this way? Are you letting a ghost from your past make you feel powerless and crippled?

While it's okay to feel that you have a negative past or a negative experience, you need to make sure that negative perception is at least based on solid facts. What are the roots of your shame, regret, or fear?

For example, after a failed speech, you might be tempted to label yourself as a poor speaker in general. That requires two causal leaps — (1) that you are a poor speaker, and (2) that the speech overall went poorly. What is your basis for believing these two things?

Are they objectively true, or is it just your subjective assessment, based in negative emotions from the one phrase you stumbled over? Often, we assess our abilities as subpar based on a negative emotion attributed to one particular folly that no one besides ourselves cared about or even noticed.

Turn to the past. Now that you can more accurately assess them — away from the influence of your emotions — how would you say your past speaking experiences have gone? Is there actually evidence and a track record to support your assumption that you are a terrible speaker? Or is there another, deeper reason for your feelings of fear and shame?

## Focus on the Moment

When you make a statement to yourself like *I'm a loser*, *nobody likes me*, or *I'm not worth talking to*, pause and give yourself time and space. Do the next four things in sequence.

First, ask yourself why you feel that way. What is the exact moment and action that caused the feeling? Is it something big, or small and isolated?

Second, what evidence is there to support that statement? Find the distortions and think about how a bystander might see the situation.

Third, think about alternate explanations for what triggered you to make that statement about yourself. Is the negative conclusion you're jumping to really what is happening? Life tends to unfold in a much simpler way than the conspiracies that get cooked up in your head.

Finally, actively think about how you can rephrase your statement about yourself the way a person with high confidence would.

A great analogy for this is when a friend or acquaintance takes a long time to respond to a text message. You might assume they're angry with you or annoyed that you wrote your text in a certain way. You might even think back through the past few weeks and come up with seven separate reasons for their being mad at you.

But if you give it enough time, go through this process, and you ask yourself certain questions, you will get a clearer picture. It's only been one hour, and they're in class or at work. You're less likely to freak out if you think these things through. You'll end up dealing with the situation the way it should be dealt with — realistically and reasonably — and you'll be happier with your conclusions.

The bottom line is simple. Dealing with negative self-talk in an unhealthy way leads to a lasting lack of confidence and self-esteem. You're just digging yourself deeper and deeper into an emotional hole. You have to arrest this process. You have to make a decision to recognize that this is not you. This is not what defines you. This is not what you're all about or capable of.

One extremely effective way to deal with inner criticism and negative self-talk is to assign a name to the "speaker" of those statements.

Bob or Beth is the negative naysayer who lives in your brain. They know nothing and are always trying to tear you down, sometimes in ridiculous ways!

*"Oh, I'm being sooo Bob right now. What about [insert your name here]? Where did he go?"*

By intellectually and emotionally disassociating yourself from this negative stream of thoughts, you can create enough logical and intellectual distance to pick apart the criticism. It no longer becomes part of who you are, so you can make progress and move beyond it. Also, this paves the way for you to more easily pick apart the internal criticisms because they are coming from someone else (Bob or Beth) and not from you.

# Chapter 14. The Zone of Mere Discomfort

Now that we've come to the end of the book, I wanted to cap it off with a chapter of action. You've read about leaving the comfort zone and even how it's an integral part of cognitive behavioral therapy. But we don't have to go from zero to therapy techniques immediately. There is certainly a wide middle ground of actions that we can start with to increase our level of confidence.

Perhaps some of these appear small or negligible, but the idea is to build up a cumulative body of work. Again, once you can create a series of victories, then your internal narrative is much more likely to skew positive rather than negative. You'll be more likely to imagine that you can do something and that you are capable because of the intentional steps you taken out of your comfort zone.

When emotions tell you one thing, it takes an exponential amount of logic to make the right decision apparent.

When you step outside your comfort zone, you must shoot for the zone of mere discomfort (and possibility), not necessarily fear or shocking the system. If you aim too high too fast, you are going to fail in spectacular fashion, which will scare you off from trying again. Therefore, you need to dip your toe outside just enough so you aren't scared witless, but enough such that you feel discomfort and uncertainty.

For example, suppose your normal rate of learning new piano songs is one song a month. To be in the zone of mere discomfort, make it a goal to learn four new songs on the piano in the next month and not 20. Imagine how much your rate of piano learning would accelerate just because you changed your perception of what was possible.

There's nothing new inside your comfort zone. Anything you pine for or that will allow you to grow lies outside. There's no magic about the people we see that seem amazingly confident and on top of the world. Their comfort zones are merely much larger than ours.

## Manipulate Your Surroundings

Realize the tangible power you can wield in the world. Manipulate your surroundings by fixing things up around the house, doing yard work, building something, or rearranging the furniture.

The point of this is to be able to visually see that you are in charge and can affect change. Take the additional step of learning the new skills involved in fixing the toilet or replacing a door. Increase your abilities and increase the amount of things you can feel confident about.

## Change Routines and Habits

Whatever you usually do on a daily basis, do something different. This can apply to all aspects of life.

Drive a different route to work. Eat at a new restaurant. Try a new coffee drink you've never had before. Eat lunch with people instead of alone at your desk. Wear shoes you haven't worn for months. Try buying a shirt in a color that is foreign to you and wear it immediately.

It's likely that you are walking in public hoping to not be noticed. Therefore, do the opposite of that as well. Try to say hello and smile to people you cross paths with, even your coworkers you see every day. You can even pair it with eye contact. It's the small forays out of your comfort zone that create the foundation you'll build upon.

Whatever actions exist in your daily life, replace them with things you have never done before.

It may seem insignificant, but the idea is to introduce uncertainty and novelty into your life. A lack of confidence comes because we imagine that there is only one path that is acceptable, and we continue to fall short of it. When you can increase your exposure and see what you might be avoiding out of habit or fear, you will be able to see it was all for nothing. Life will never be as your plan, and altering your habits and routines lets you feel the comfort in discomfort and uncertainty.

**Practice Assertiveness**

Assertiveness is a scary prospect for most people because we feel that it will lead to unnecessary confrontation and embarrassing results for us. This might be true around 1% of the time. What happens the rest of the 99% of the time when you assert yourself? You either get what you want or receive a polite no. That's not so bad.

Practicing assertiveness is getting used to the feeling of imminent rejection, no matter how small. For example, asking for a discount or coupon the next time you are at any store — a retailer, grocery store, or even restaurant. It's likely your request will be rejected, but what is the worst that will happen? You'll feel awkward to be sure, and you get become red-faced, but that's as bad as it will get. You will have actually created an awkward situation, and then by the end of it, no one will have punished you or ridiculed you. It's simply over.

That's a conundrum of living outside your comfort zone. You may feel tension from feelings of imminent rejection from time to time, but it also doesn't matter because you'll have grown accustomed to them and desensitized, in a way.

Another easy way to be more assertive is to proactively plan and arrange outings for your friends or family — for instance, taking the lead on coordinating all the details for a weekend lake trip. This is massively beneficial in two ways. First, you are going to grow your planning and arranging skills, which will give you another ability to be confident in and hang your hat on. If you've planned a weekend trip for 15 people, including food and transportation, that's no small feat and makes other occasions feel easier.

Second, it puts you into the self-assigned role of the boss, the leader. Suddenly, you're not *you*, you're in a role regarding the planning. People will defer to you and you will feel confident in asking others to do things for you. You're the one who knows best, and it's amazing how having a reason to talk, interact, and ask people questions will make you feel powerful and confident. Make sure to stop the group to take photos as well, as this will help you exercise additional confidence.

If you are already in this planning or supervisory role, then take the opposite approach and allow friends and family to make plans for you. Remember, take what you usually do and do the opposite. This will likely give you an extreme sense of discomfort because there will be uncertainty, but you'll find that you can put yourself in a situation where you don't know what to expect and come out just fine.

## Jump

Finally, you can just take a leap of faith and confront a fear head-on. Look at it straight in the eye and laugh at it. Jump out of a plane or go to a spider zoo. Whatever it is, it should make you extremely uncomfortable — not because it's inherently uncomfortable, but because it evokes fear in you.

This defies the concept of the zone of mere discomfort, but some people just need to jump in. They can't simply dip their toe in the water because it will be too little progress and they will never able to change their internal narratives with it.

So jump. Say yes to whatever you come across and make it a policy to never turn anything down. Does it feel like you are saying yes to everything? It's probably because you have been subconsciously programmed to say no to everything without realizing it. Take the opportunities and chances that lead directly out of your comfort zone and far past the zone of mere discomfort. Inoculate yourself to fear, build up your tolerance, and recognize the only boundaries are in your head. Prioritize simple action.

## Conclusion

Here's hoping that you have gained a realistic and healthy perspective on what it means to be truly confident.

As I stated before, however, it's not just a matter of magically reading a book and embodying those special mindsets. Recall that it's nearly impossible to logic confidence into existence. It is instead built by action and staring fear in the face.

Realizing and accepting this will put you ahead of 99% of people who wish to change themselves. If you keep doing what you've always done, you'll keep getting what you've always gotten. This can be good or bad news for you; I'll let you decide which.

Sincerely,

Patrick King
Social Interaction Specialist and Conversation Coach
www.PatrickKingConsulting.com

P.S.: If you enjoyed this book, please don't be shy and drop me a line, leave a review, or both! I love reading feedback, and reviews are the lifeblood of Kindle books, so they are always welcome and greatly appreciated.

## Speaking and Coaching

Imagine going far beyond the contents of this book and dramatically improving the way you interact with the world, as well as the relationships you'll build.

Are you interested in contacting Patrick for ...

- ... a social skills workshop for your workplace?
- ... speaking engagements on the power of conversation and charisma?
- ... personalized social skills and conversation coaching?

Patrick speaks around the world to help people improve their lives through the power of building relationships with improved social skills. He is a recognized industry expert, bestselling author, and speaker.

To invite Patrick to speak at your next event or to inquire about coaching, get in touch directly through his website's contact form at http://www.PatrickKingConsulting.com/contact, or contact him directly at Patrick@patrickkingconsulting.com.

**Cheat Sheet**

Before devouring the cheat sheet, remember, as a **FREE** show of appreciation to my readers, I've put together The Flawless Interaction Checklist. It describes in-depth the 7 essential components to exceptional interactions and conversations, from strangers to relationships and everything in-between.

**Including how to:** make people comfortable, connect easily, develop killer eye contact, prepare for any social situation, look like a mind reader, and never run out of things to say. Click over to download your FREE copy now!

**Chapter 1. The Gatekeeper**

Confidence is the singular which that will allow you to take life on your own terms, otherwise you will be driven by fear and anxiety.

## Chapter 2. Diagnose Triggers

We all have triggers, sometimes subconscious, that cause us to feel a lack of confidence. Fear creeps in and changes our mindsets without us realizing it.

## Chapter 3. Imposter Syndrome

Imposter syndrome is when you feel you don't belong because you are inadequate, incompetent, or simply stupid. All of us feel this to some degree, and it's because we react emotionally instead of looking at the evidence of our positives.

## Chapter 4. The Life-Changing Magic of *Doing*

Reading and talking about confidence is helpful, but ultimately, confidence springs from action. Simply doing is the key to feeling better about yourself and understanding realistic consequences.

## Chapter 5. Take Inventory

Look at yourself and take inventory of your strengths and weaknesses from an objective standpoint. Change the narrative that you are incapable and inadequate.

## Chapter 6. The Myth of Perfection

No one is perfect, which is a good thing because perfection is intimidating. Perfectionism is a mental disease that occurs not because you have high standards, but because you are afraid of the judgment that will follow if you come up short.

## Chapter 7. Prepare to Perform

If you are preparing for a big speech, you would prepare with repetition and focus. What else can you apply that to?

## Chapter 8. Look in the Mirror

One of the easiest ways to improve confidence is to improve your exterior. Sorry, but that's life. Reap the rewards of more positive feedback from how you look and the rest will follow.

**Chapter 9. Mindsets**

There are specific thought patterns you should use on a daily basis, as well as those to absolutely avoid whenever possible. "Settle" more, feel gratitude, and measure your effort and not your results.

**Chapter 10. Get Stoic**

Stoicism allows you to take obstacles and low confidence and turn them upside down. Events are neutral and emotions are human-made, so it is your choice how to respond to them.

**Chapter 11. Supreme Self-Esteem**

Self-esteem is composed of self-respect and self-efficacy, and as well Branden's six pillars.

**Chapter 12. Cognitive Confidence**

Cognitive behavioral therapy is aimed at changing people's thought and behavior patterns in regards to low confidence. Popular methods include cognitive restructuring and systematic exposure.

## Chapter 13. Banish Your Negative Self-Talk

You likely evaluate the world in a negative way and expect to be treated poorly. This begins with how you talk to yourself and the narrative your self-talk creates.

## Chapter 14. The Zone of Mere Discomfort

If you keep doing what you've always done, you'll keep getting the results you've always gotten. Is this positive or negative for you? You must step out of your comfort zone bit by bit to experience actual change.

## DATE DUE

Made in the USA
Columbia, SC
11 February 2019